NELSON
MANDELA

BY EMANUEL CASTRO   ILLUSTRATED BY IGNACIO SEGESSO

CAPSTONE PRESS
a capstone imprint

Graphic Library is published by Capstone Press,
1710 Roe Crest Drive, North Mankato, Minnesota 56003
www.mycapstone.com

Cataloging-in-Publication Data is available at the Library
of Congress website.
ISBN 978-1-5157-9164-5 (library binding)
ISBN 978-1-5157-9168-3 (paperback)
ISBN 978-1-5157-9172-0 (eBook PDF)

Summary: Follow Nelson Mandela's life as he evolves from
lawyer to leader in this unofficial biography.

Author: Emanuel Castro
Illustrator: Ignacio Segesso

Translated into the English language by
Trusted Translations

Printed in China.
0483

TABLE OF CONTENTS

CHAPTER 1
THE OTHER AFRICA

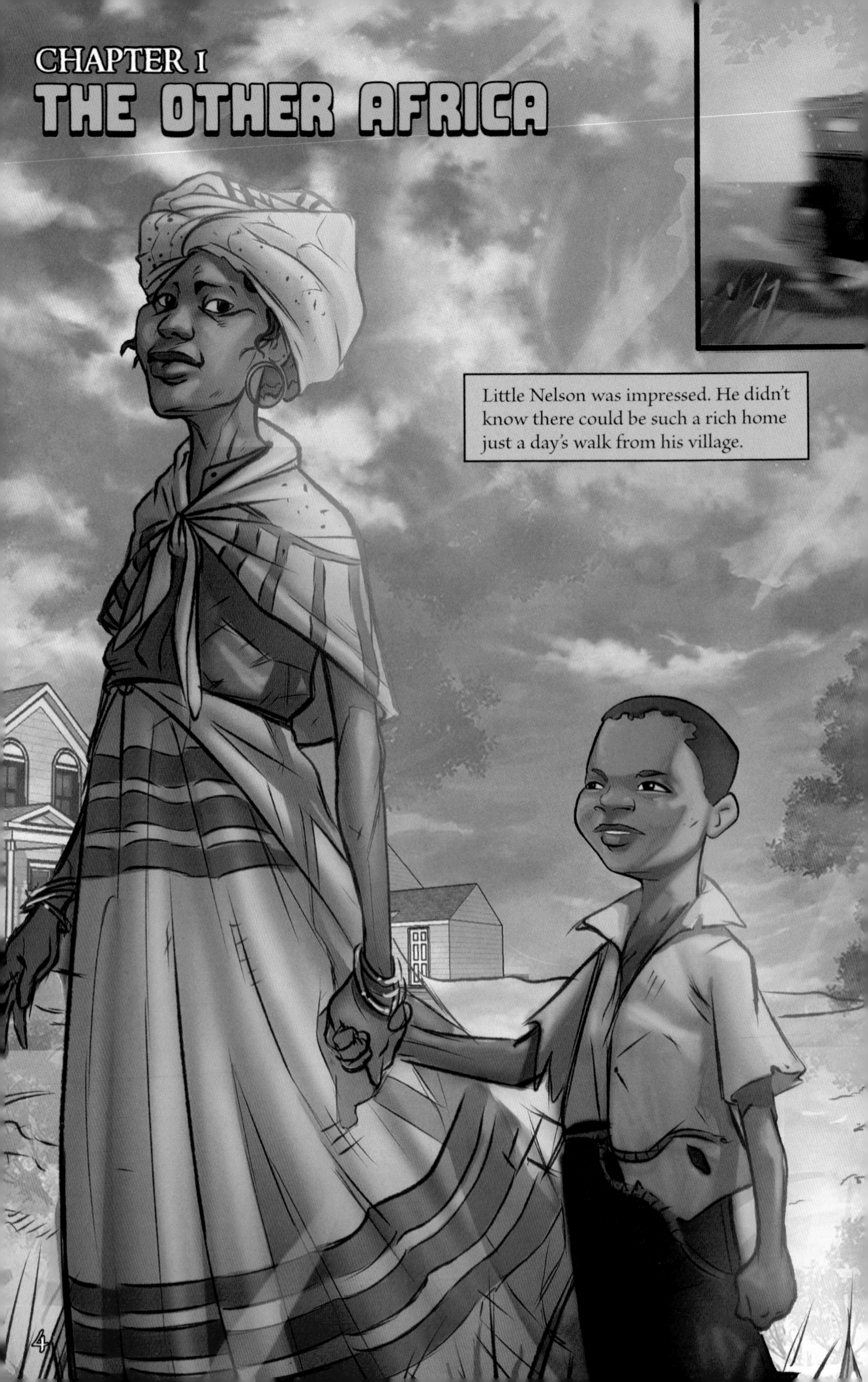
Little Nelson was impressed. He didn't know there could be such a rich home just a day's walk from his village.

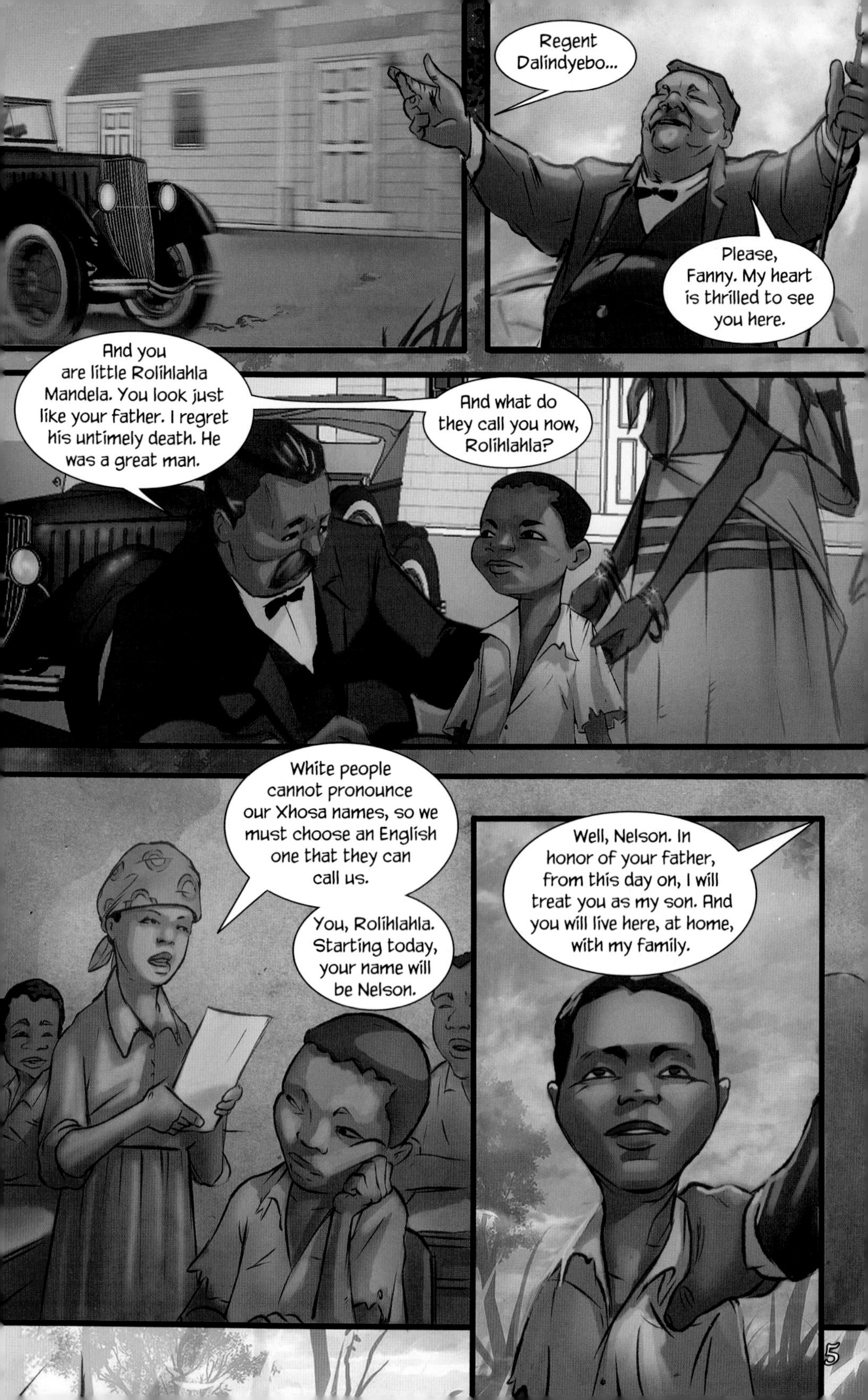
Regent Dalindyebo...
Please, Fanny. My heart is thrilled to see you here.
And you are little Rolihlahla Mandela. You look just like your father. I regret his untimely death. He was a great man.
And what do they call you now, Rolihlahla?
White people cannot pronounce our Xhosa names, so we must choose an English one that they can call us.
You, Rolihlahla. Starting today, your name will be Nelson.
Well, Nelson. In honor of your father, from this day on, I will treat you as my son. And you will live here, at home, with my family.

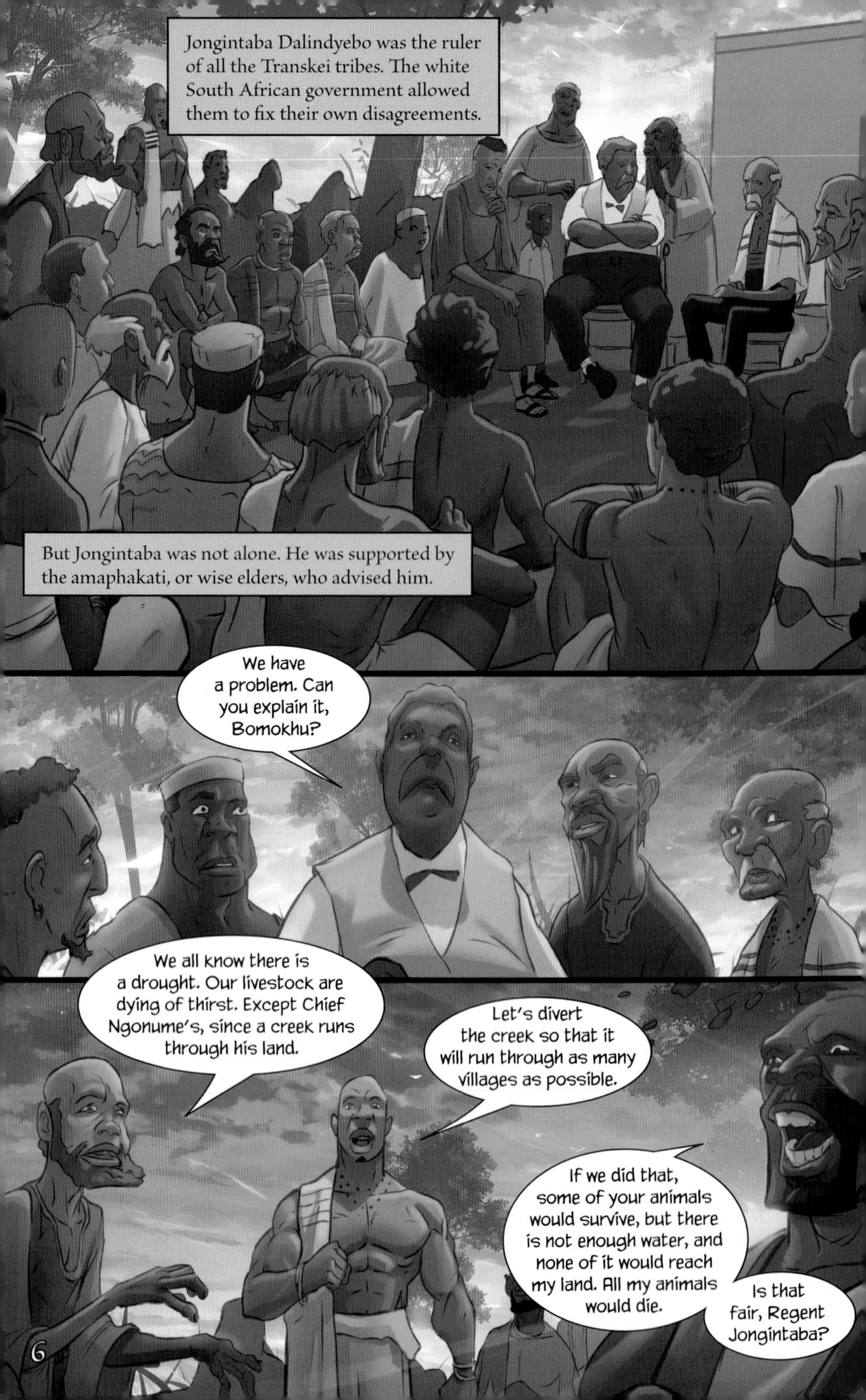

Jongintaba Dalindyebo was the ruler of all the Transkei tribes. The white South African government allowed them to fix their own disagreements.
But Jongintaba was not alone. He was supported by the amaphakati, or wise elders, who advised him.
We have a problem. Can you explain it, Bomokhu?
We all know there is a drought. Our livestock are dying of thirst. Except Chief Ngonume's, since a creek runs through his land.
Let's divert the creek so that it will run through as many villages as possible.
If we did that, some of your animals would survive, but there is not enough water, and none of it would reach my land. All my animals would die.
Is that fair, Regent Jongintaba?

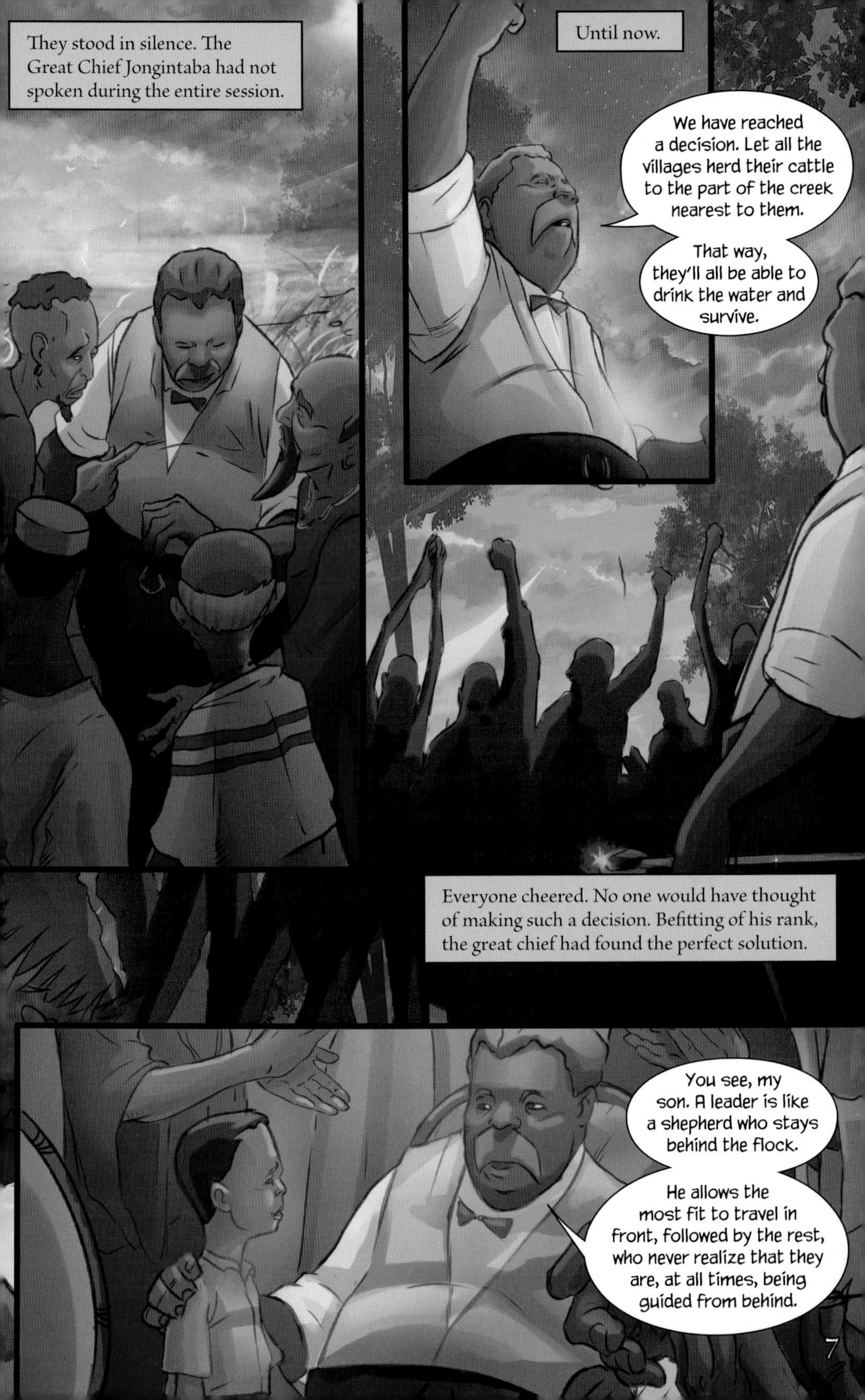

They stood in silence. The Great Chief Jongintaba had not spoken during the entire session.
Until now.
We have reached a decision. Let all the villages herd their cattle to the part of the creek nearest to them.
That way, they'll all be able to drink the water and survive.
Everyone cheered. No one would have thought of making such a decision. Befitting of his rank, the great chief had found the perfect solution.
You see, my son. A leader is like a shepherd who stays behind the flock.
He allows the most fit to travel in front, followed by the rest, who never realize that they are, at all times, being guided from behind.

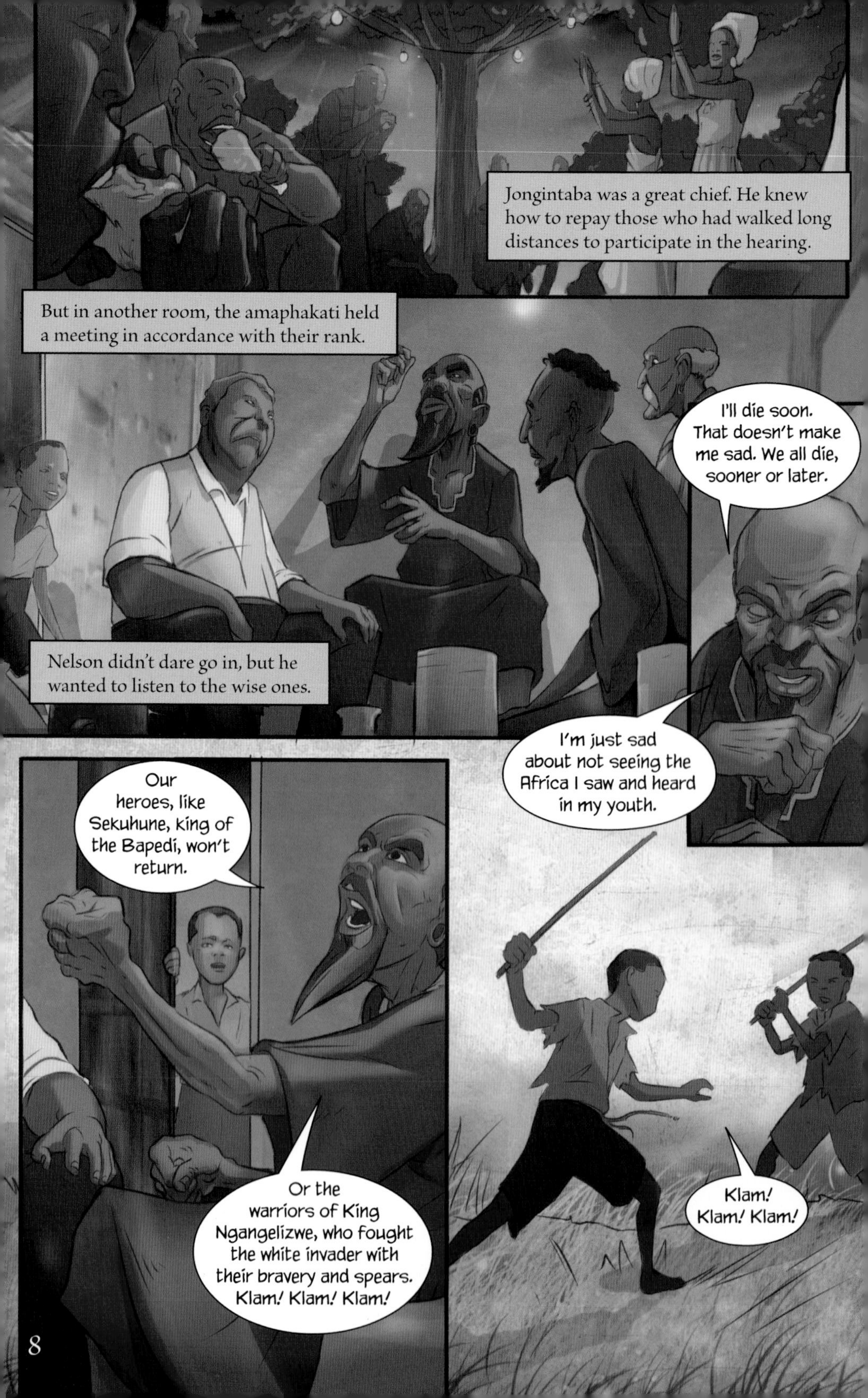

Jongintaba was a great chief. He knew how to repay those who had walked long distances to participate in the hearing.
But in another room, the amaphakati held a meeting in accordance with their rank.
Nelson didn't dare go in, but he wanted to listen to the wise ones.
I'll die soon. That doesn't make me sad. We all die, sooner or later.
I'm just sad about not seeing the Africa I saw and heard in my youth.
Our heroes, like Sekuhune, king of the Bapedi, won't return.
Or the warriors of King Ngangelizwe, who fought the white invader with their bravery and spears. Klam! Klam! Klam!
Klam! Klam! Klam!

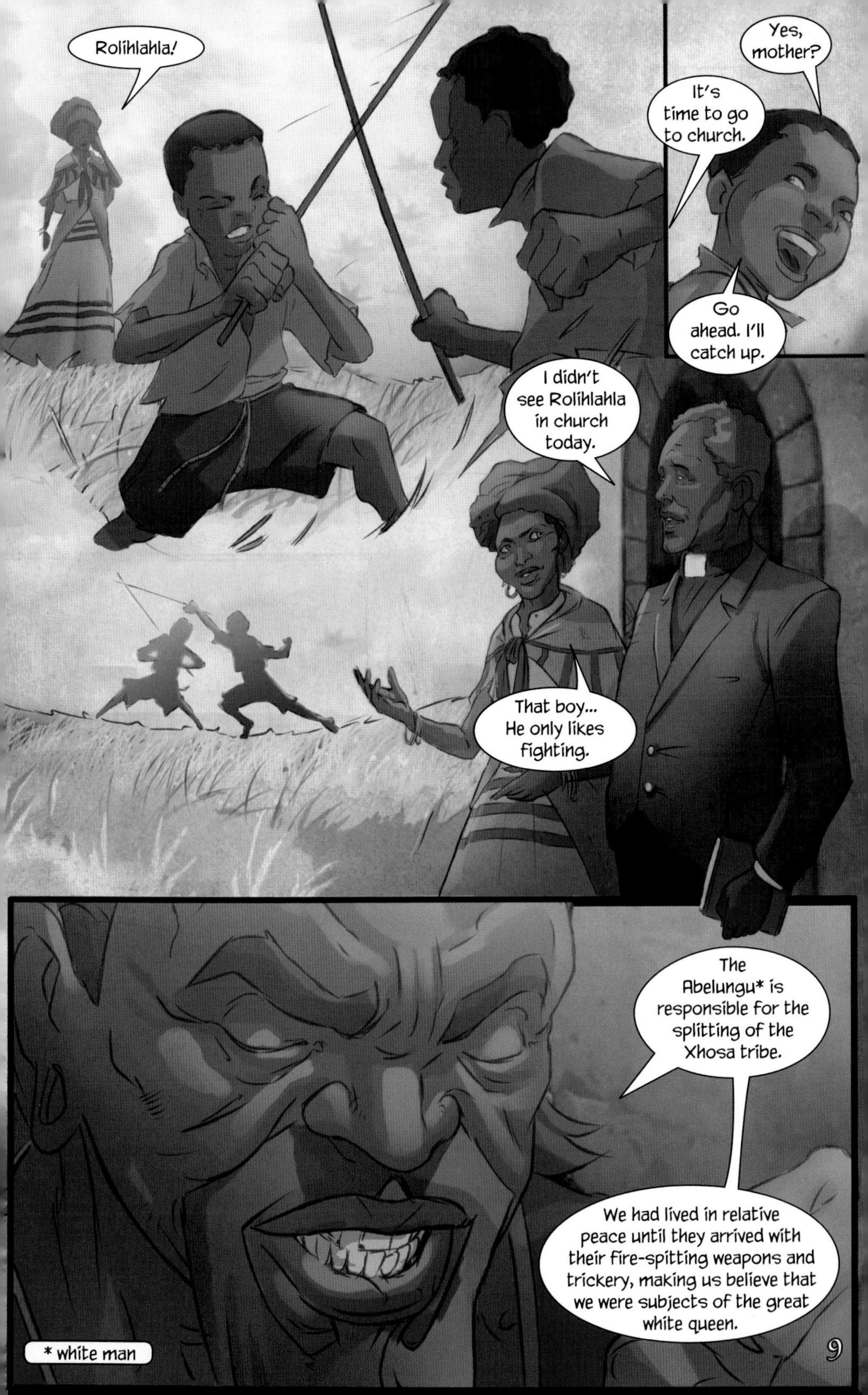

Rolihlahla!
Yes, mother?
It's time to go to church.
Go ahead. I'll catch up.
I didn't see Rolihlahla in church today.
That boy... He only likes fighting.
The Abelungu* is responsible for the splitting of the Xhosa tribe.
We had lived in relative peace until they arrived with their fire-spitting weapons and trickery, making us believe that we were subjects of the great white queen.
* white man

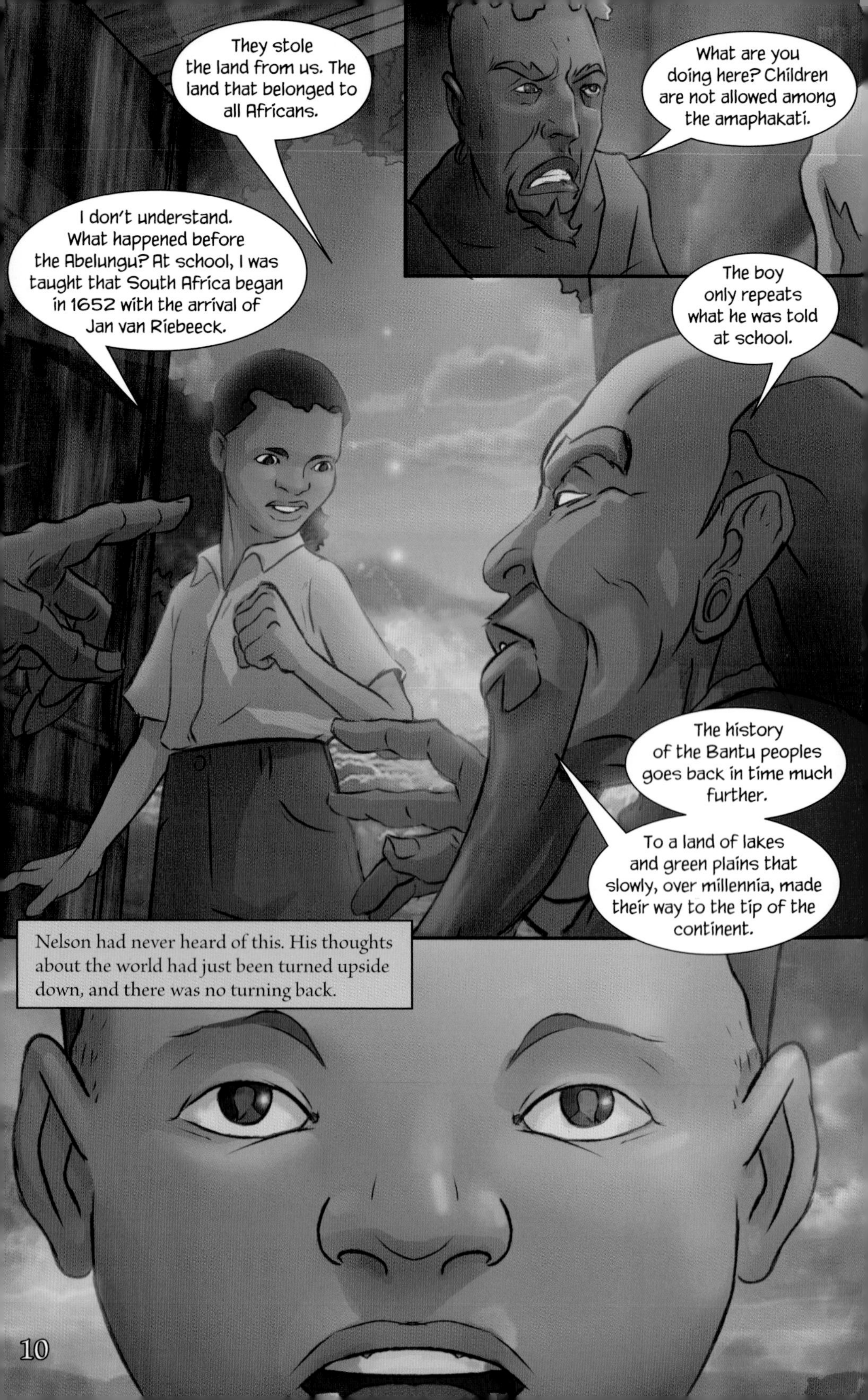
They stole the land from us. The land that belonged to all Africans.
What are you doing here? Children are not allowed among the amaphakati.
I don't understand. What happened before the Abelungu? At school, I was taught that South Africa began in 1652 with the arrival of Jan van Riebeeck.
The boy only repeats what he was told at school.
The history of the Bantu peoples goes back in time much further.
To a land of lakes and green plains that slowly, over millennia, made their way to the tip of the continent.
Nelson had never heard of this. His thoughts about the world had just been turned upside down, and there was no turning back.

CHAPTER 2
RADICAL WORDS

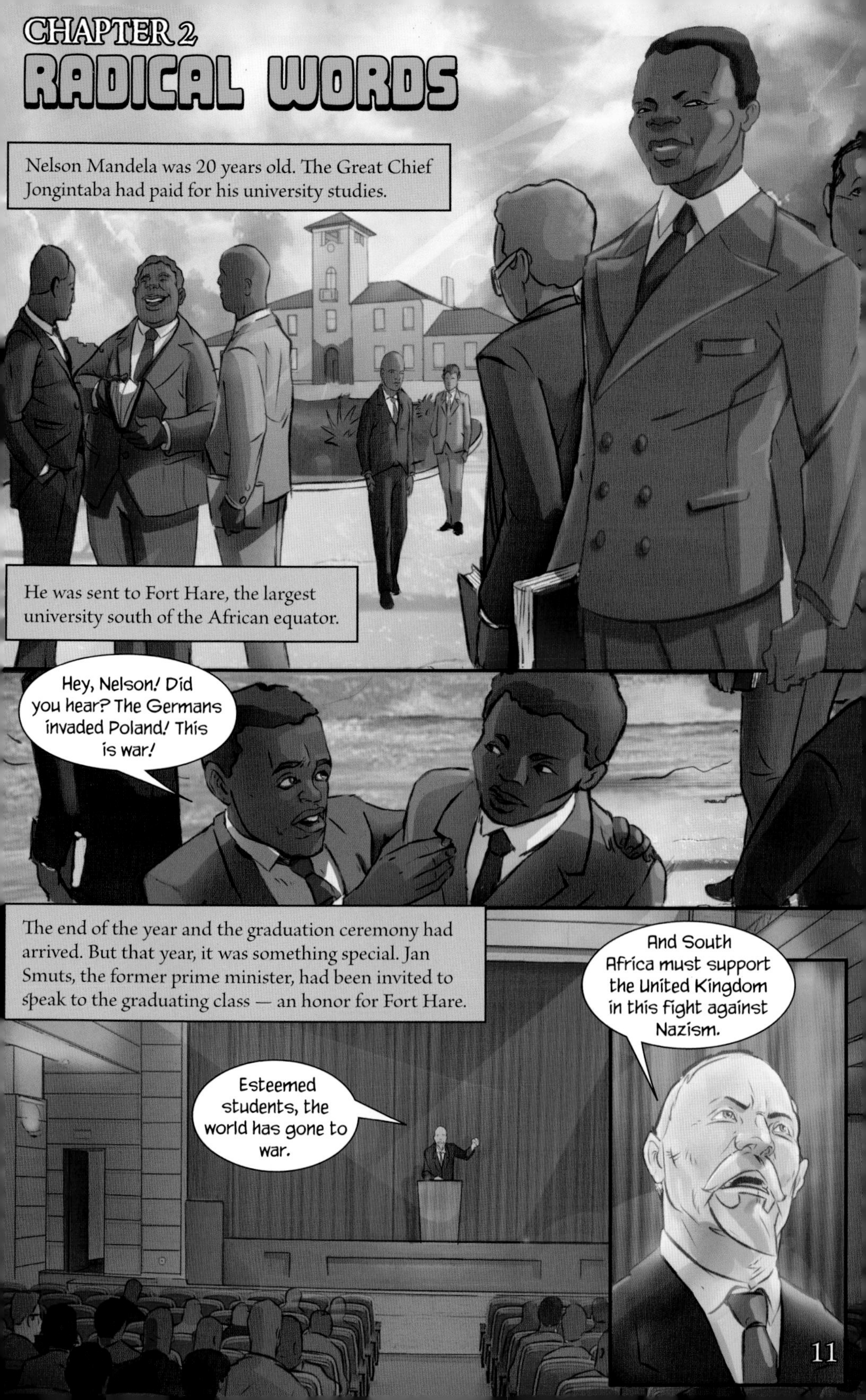
Nelson Mandela was 20 years old. The Great Chief Jongintaba had paid for his university studies.
He was sent to Fort Hare, the largest university south of the African equator.
Hey, Nelson! Did you hear? The Germans invaded Poland! This is war!
The end of the year and the graduation ceremony had arrived. But that year, it was something special. Jan Smuts, the former prime minister, had been invited to speak to the graduating class — an honor for Fort Hare.
Esteemed students, the world has gone to war.
And South Africa must support the United Kingdom in this fight against Nazism.

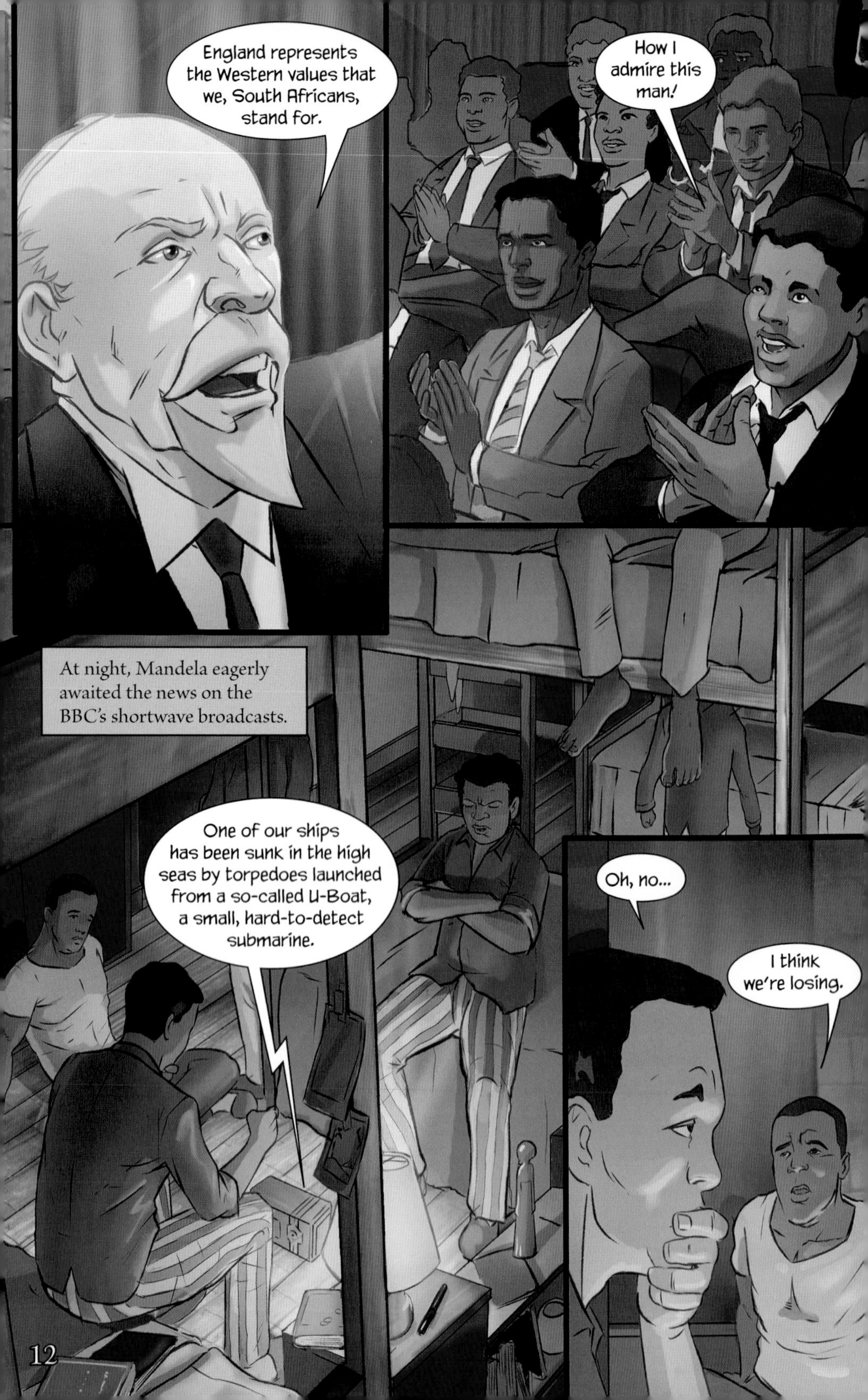
England represents the Western values that we, South Africans, stand for.
How I admire this man!
At night, Mandela eagerly awaited the news on the BBC's shortwave broadcasts.
One of our ships has been sunk in the high seas by torpedoes launched from a so-called U-Boat, a small, hard-to-detect submarine.
Oh, no...
I think we're losing.

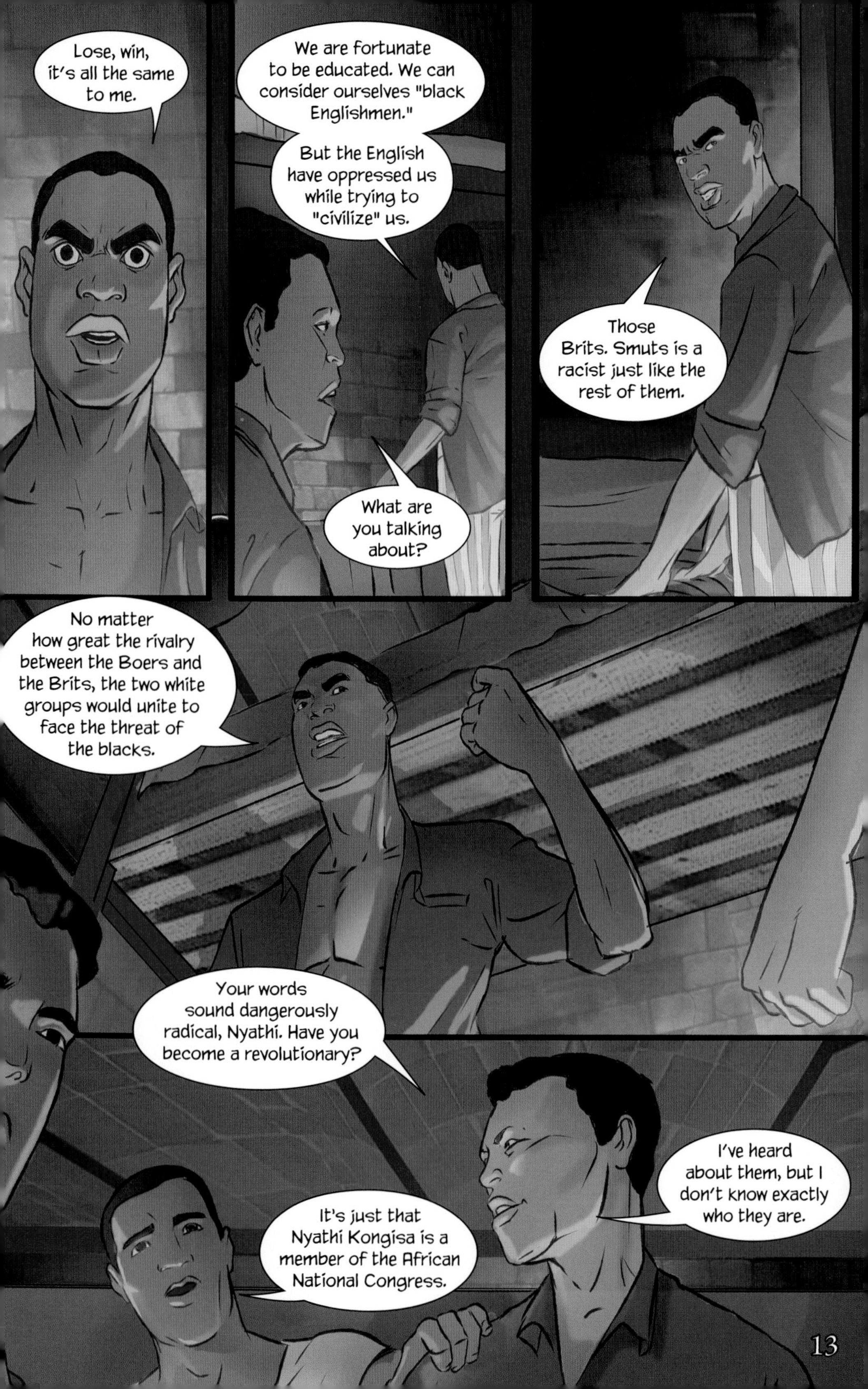
Lose, win, it's all the same to me.
We are fortunate to be educated. We can consider ourselves "black Englishmen."
But the English have oppressed us while trying to "civilize" us.
What are you talking about?
Those Brits. Smuts is a racist just like the rest of them.
No matter how great the rivalry between the Boers and the Brits, the two white groups would unite to face the threat of the blacks.
Your words sound dangerously radical, Nyathi. Have you become a revolutionary?
It's just that Nyathi Kongisa is a member of the African National Congress.
I've heard about them, but I don't know exactly who they are.

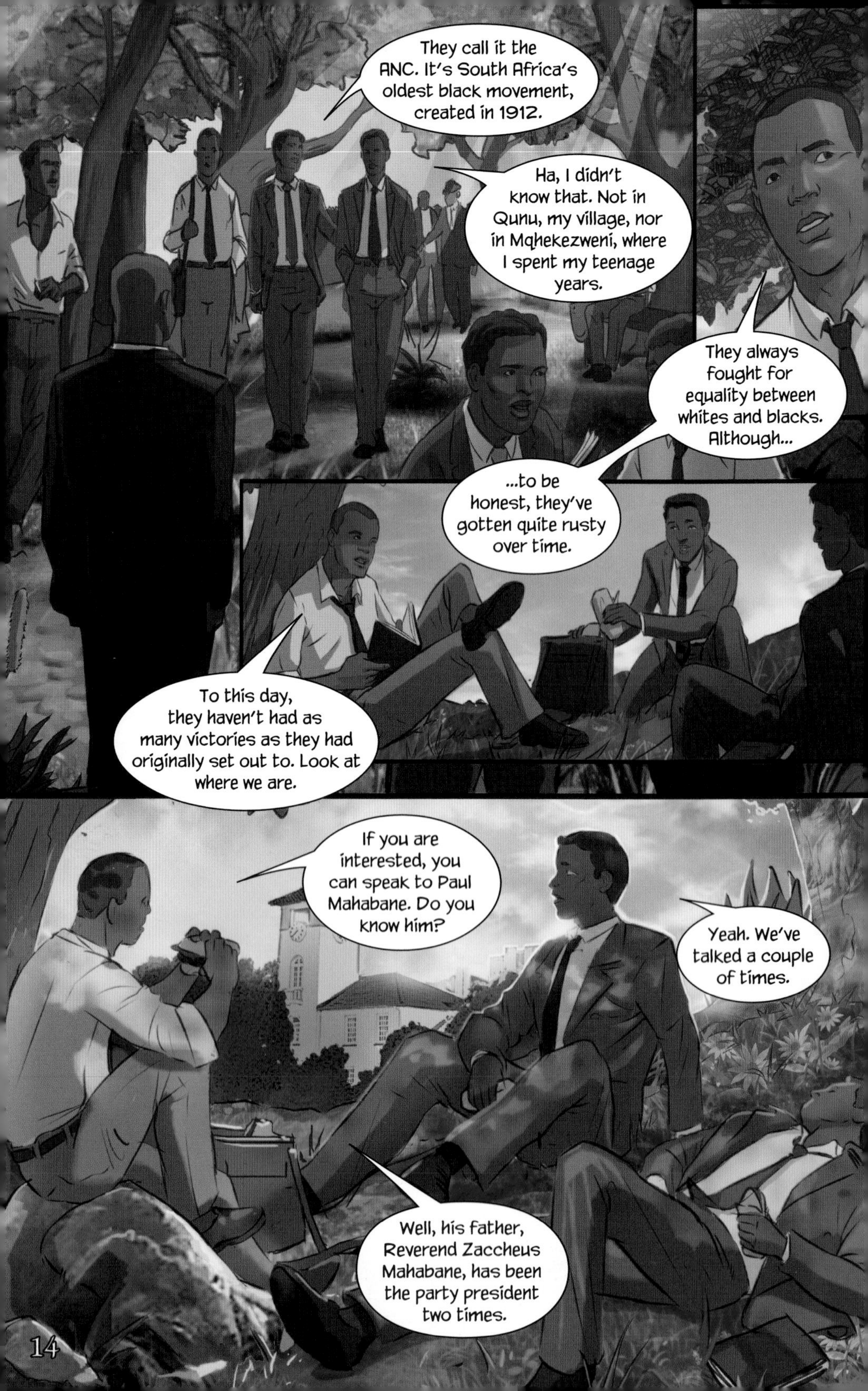
They call it the ANC. It's South Africa's oldest black movement, created in 1912.
Ha, I didn't know that. Not in Qunu, my village, nor in Mqhekezweni, where I spent my teenage years.
They always fought for equality between whites and blacks. Although...
...to be honest, they've gotten quite rusty over time.
To this day, they haven't had as many victories as they had originally set out to. Look at where we are.
If you are interested, you can speak to Paul Mahabane. Do you know him?
Yeah. We've talked a couple of times.
Well, his father, Reverend Zaccheus Mahabane, has been the party president two times.

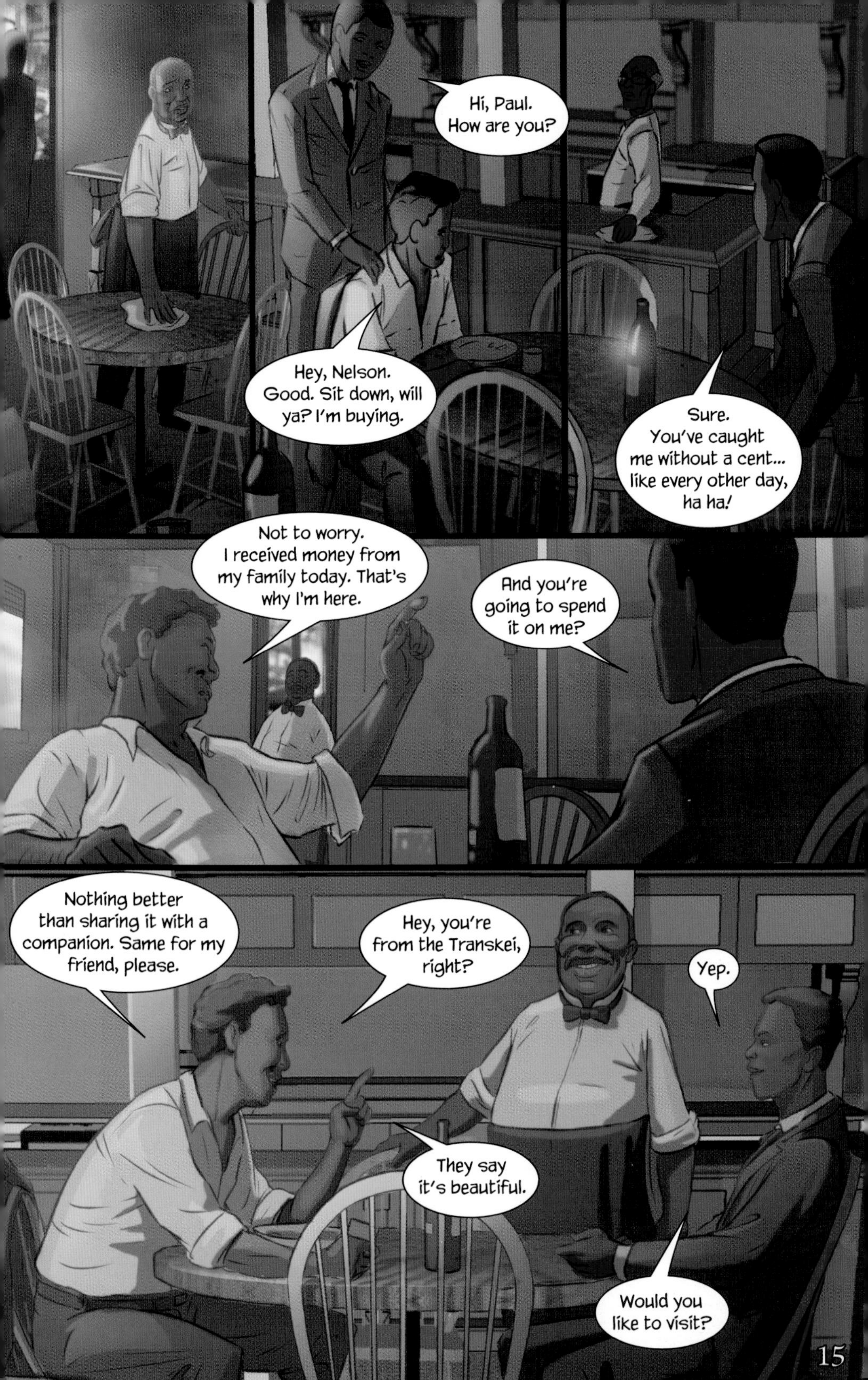
Hi, Paul.
How are you?
Hey, Nelson.
Good. Sit down, will
ya? I'm buying.
Sure.
You've caught
me without a cent...
like every other day,
ha ha!
Not to worry.
I received money from
my family today. That's
why I'm here.
And you're
going to spend
it on me?
Nothing better
than sharing it with a
companion. Same for my
friend, please.
Hey, you're
from the Transkei,
right?
Yep.
They say
it's beautiful.
Would you
like to visit?

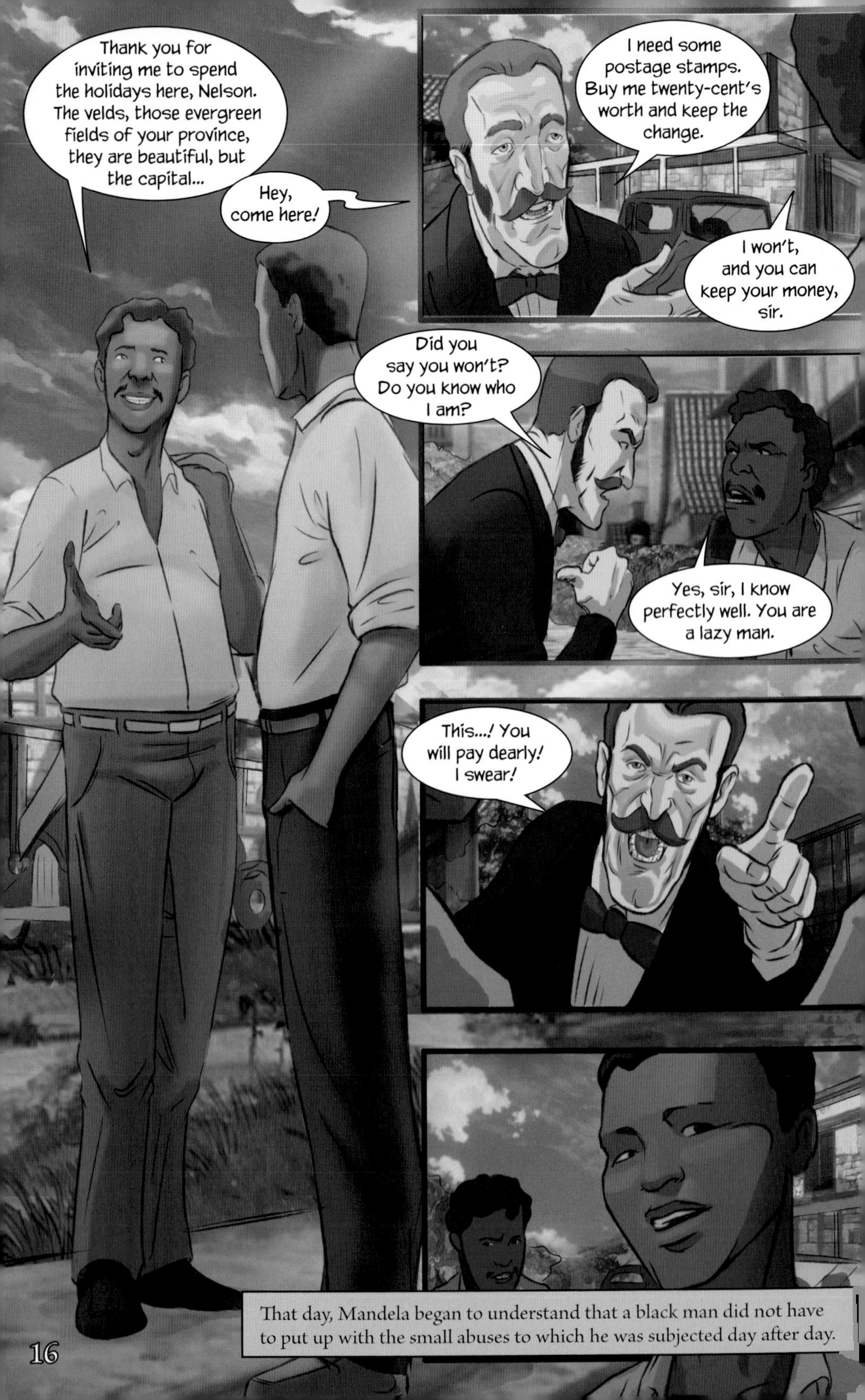
Thank you for inviting me to spend the holidays here, Nelson. The velds, those evergreen fields of your province, they are beautiful, but the capital...
Hey, come here!
I need some postage stamps. Buy me twenty-cent's worth and keep the change.
I won't, and you can keep your money, sir.
Did you say you won't? Do you know who I am?
Yes, sir, I know perfectly well. You are a lazy man.
This...! You will pay dearly! I swear!
That day, Mandela began to understand that a black man did not have to put up with the small abuses to which he was subjected day after day.

CHAPTER 3
A BETTER COUNTRY

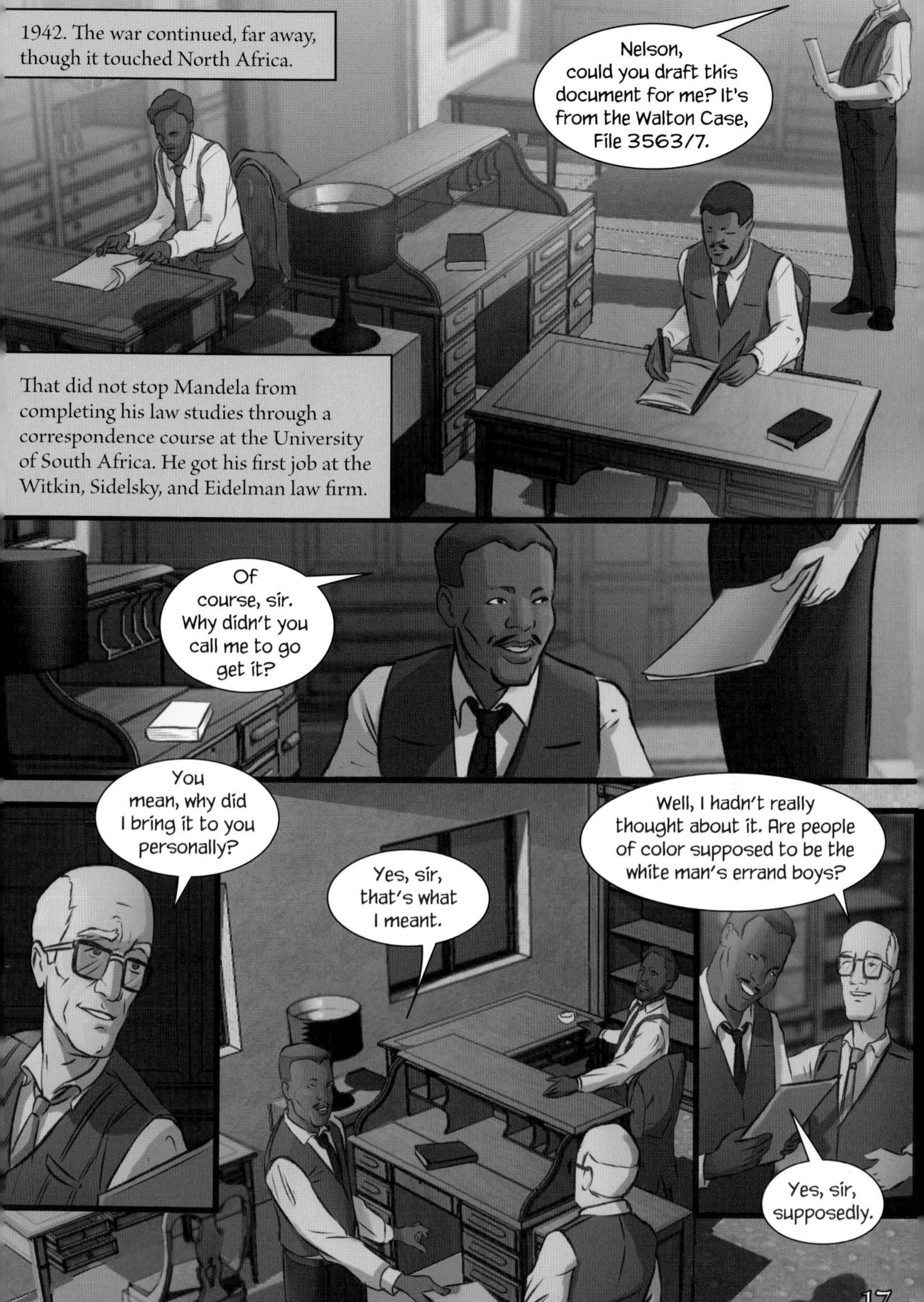
1942. The war continued, far away, though it touched North Africa.
Nelson, could you draft this document for me? It's from the Walton Case, File 3563/7.
That did not stop Mandela from completing his law studies through a correspondence course at the University of South Africa. He got his first job at the Witkin, Sidelsky, and Eidelman law firm.
Of course, sir. Why didn't you call me to go get it?
You mean, why did I bring it to you personally?
Yes, sir, that's what I meant.
Well, I hadn't really thought about it. Are people of color supposed to be the white man's errand boys?
Yes, sir, supposedly.

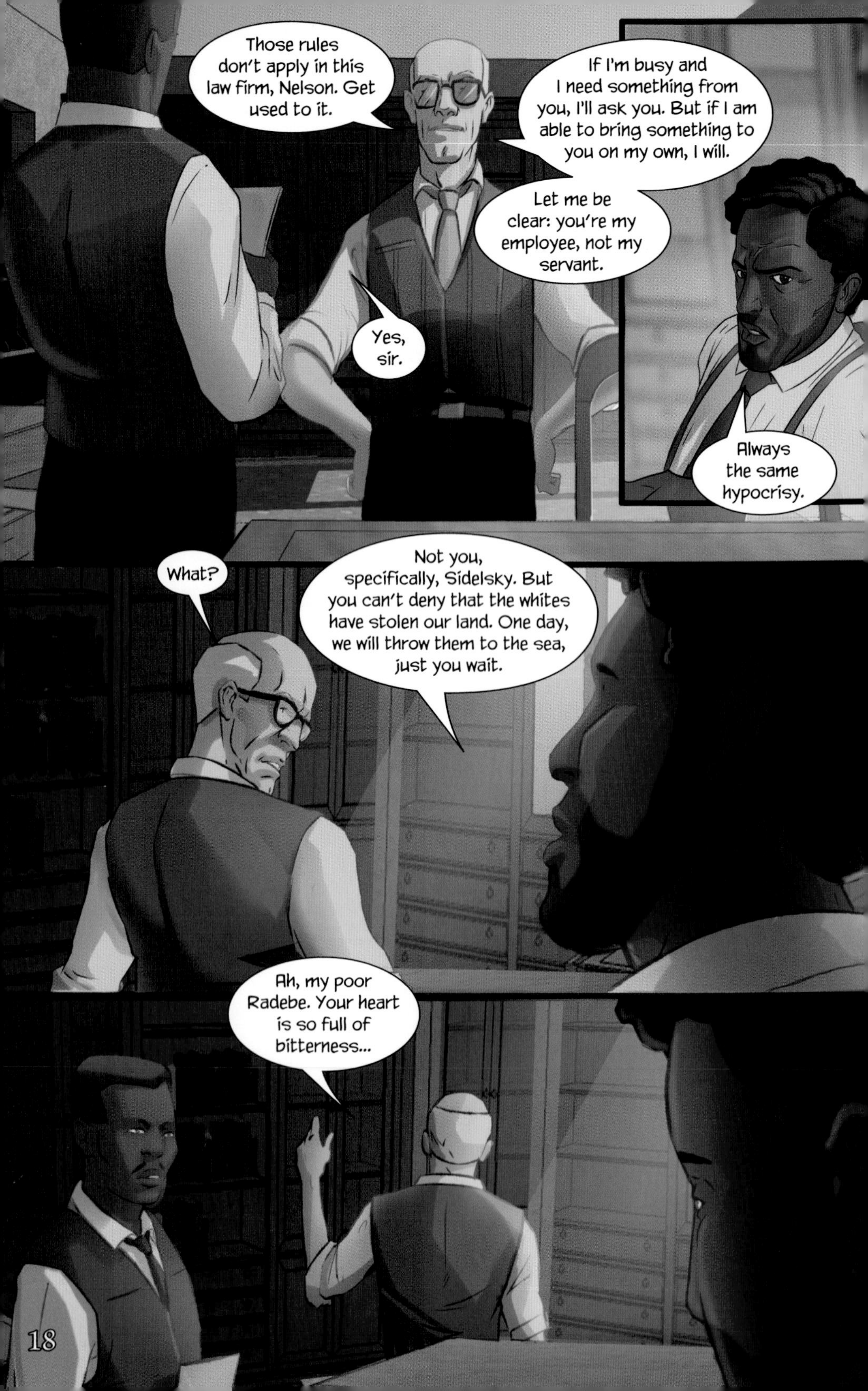
Those rules don't apply in this law firm, Nelson. Get used to it.
If I'm busy and I need something from you, I'll ask you. But if I am able to bring something to you on my own, I will.
Let me be clear: you're my employee, not my servant.
Yes, sir.
Always the same hypocrisy.
What?
Not you, specifically, Sidelsky. But you can't deny that the whites have stolen our land. One day, we will throw them to the sea, just you wait.
Ah, my poor Radebe. Your heart is so full of bitterness...

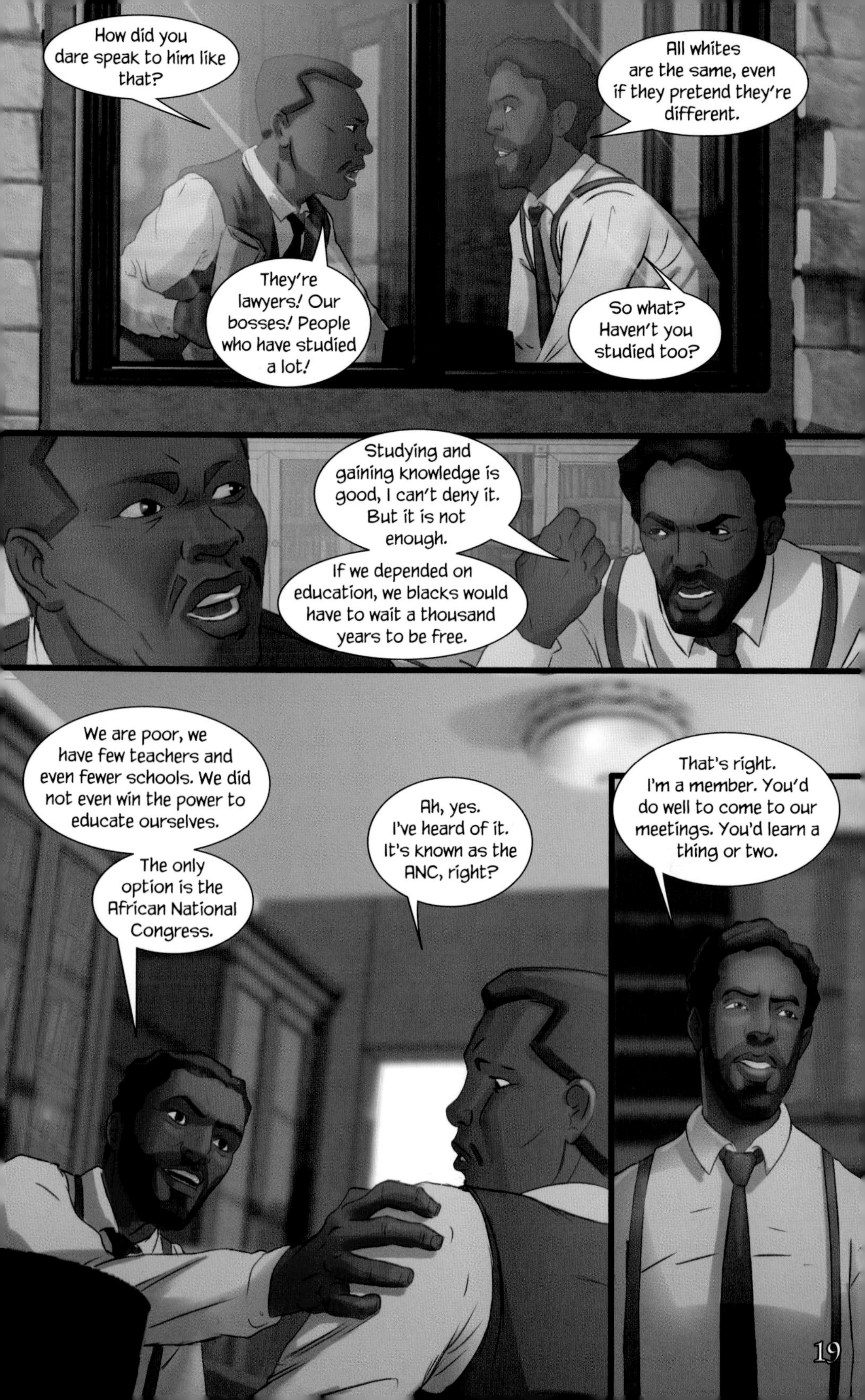
How did you dare speak to him like that?
All whites are the same, even if they pretend they're different.
They're lawyers! Our bosses! People who have studied a lot!
So what? Haven't you studied too?
Studying and gaining knowledge is good, I can't deny it. But it is not enough.
If we depended on education, we blacks would have to wait a thousand years to be free.
We are poor, we have few teachers and even fewer schools. We did not even win the power to educate ourselves.
The only option is the African National Congress.
Ah, yes. I've heard of it. It's known as the ANC, right?
That's right. I'm a member. You'd do well to come to our meetings. You'd learn a thing or two.

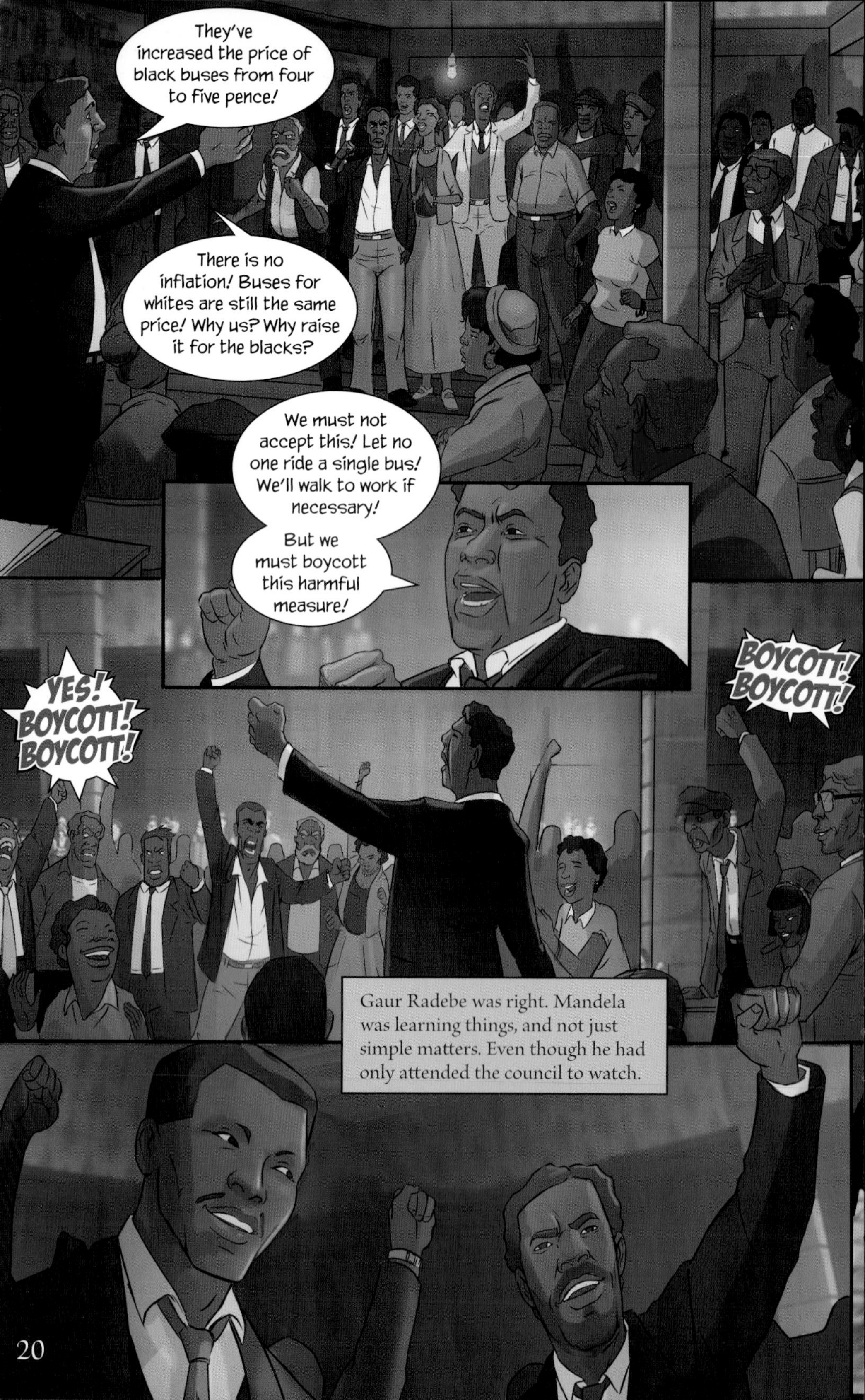

They've increased the price of black buses from four to five pence!
There is no inflation! Buses for whites are still the same price! Why us? Why raise it for the blacks?
We must not accept this! Let no one ride a single bus! We'll walk to work if necessary!
But we must boycott this harmful measure!
YES! BOYCOTT! BOYCOTT!
BOYCOTT! BOYCOTT!
Gaur Radebe was right. Mandela was learning things, and not just simple matters. Even though he had only attended the council to watch.

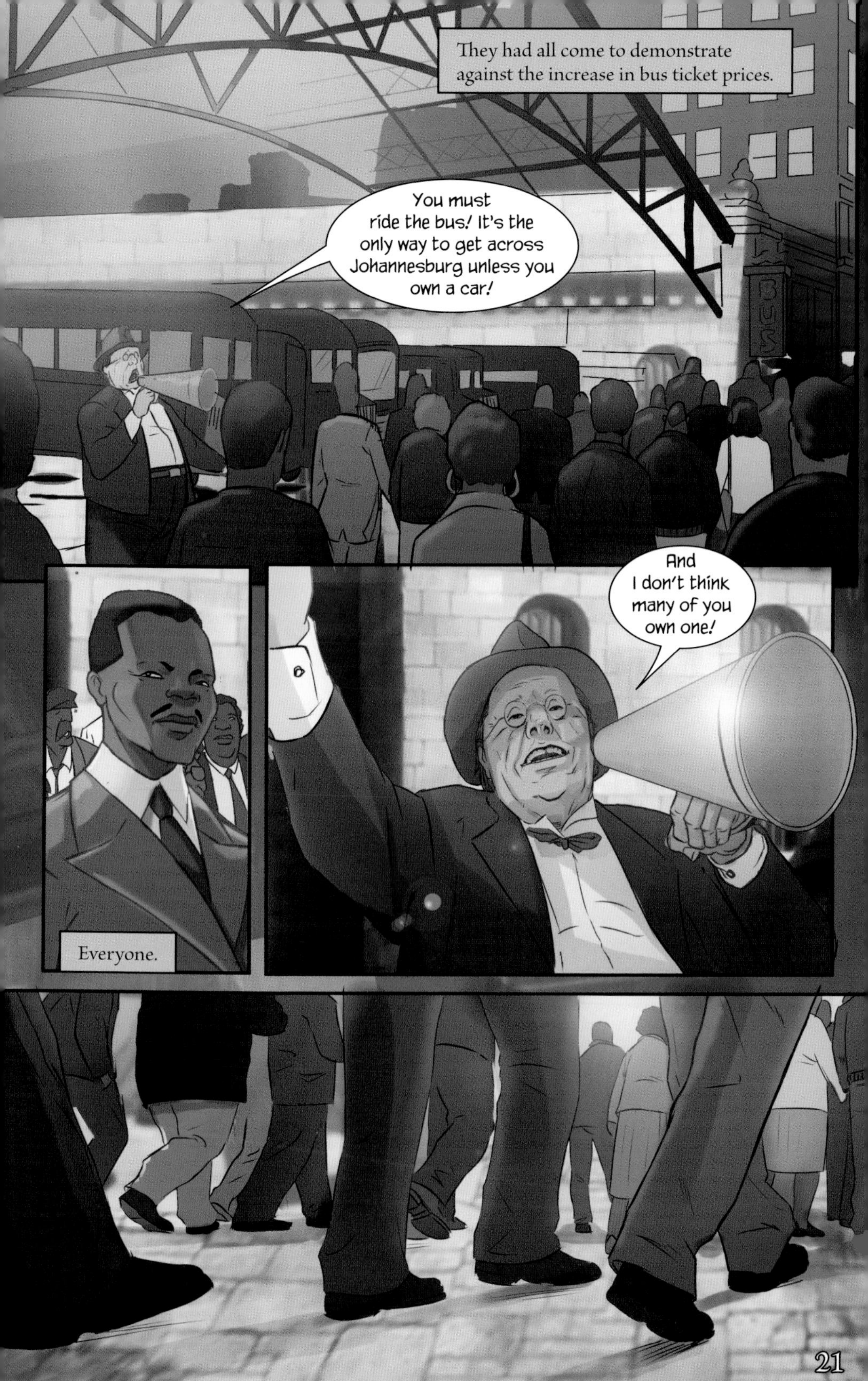
They had all come to demonstrate against the increase in bus ticket prices.
You must ride the bus! It's the only way to get across Johannesburg unless you own a car!
BUS
Everyone.
And I don't think many of you own one!

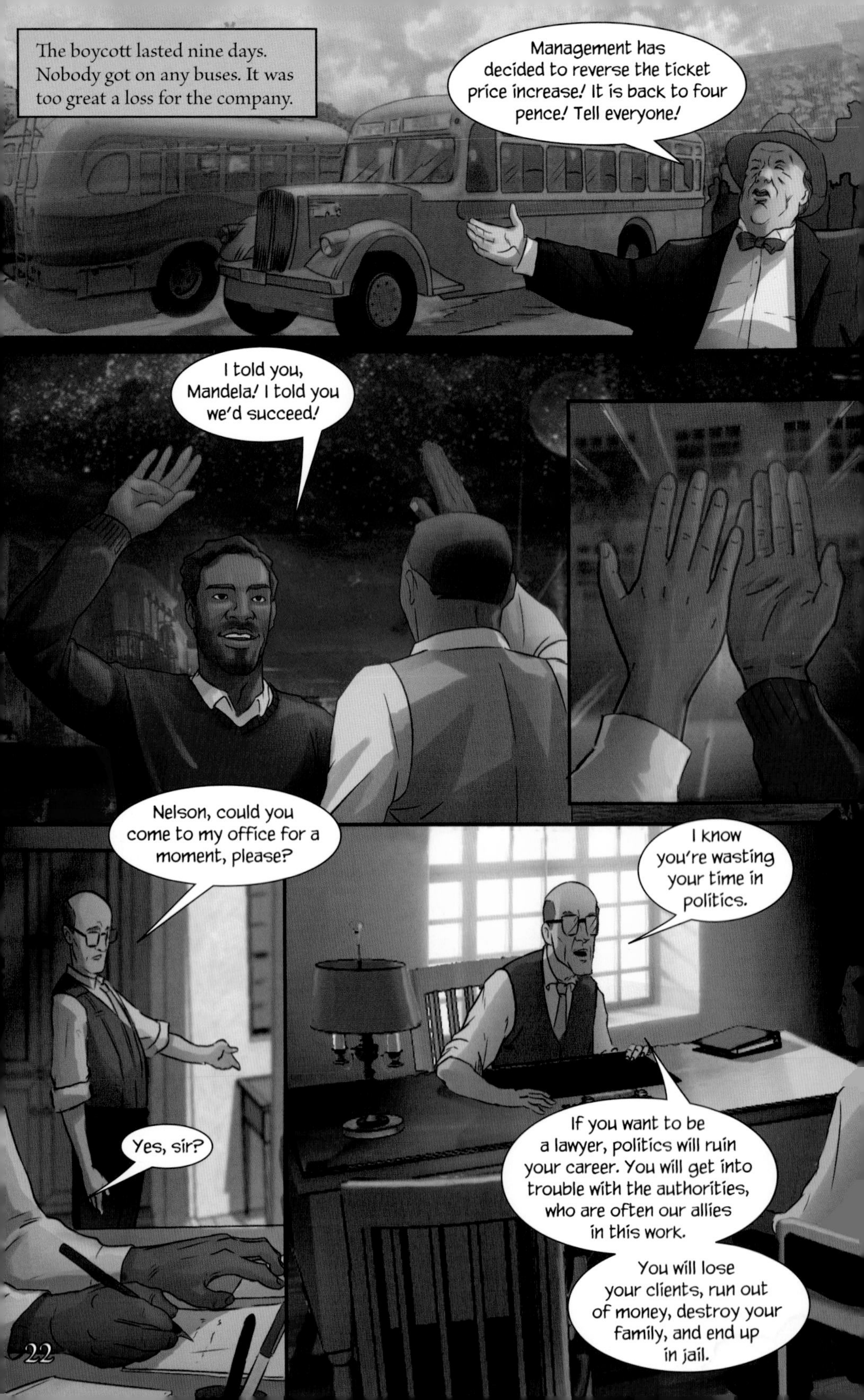
The boycott lasted nine days. Nobody got on any buses. It was too great a loss for the company.
Management has decided to reverse the ticket price increase! It is back to four pence! Tell everyone!
I told you, Mandela! I told you we'd succeed!
Nelson, could you come to my office for a moment, please?
Yes, sir?
I know you're wasting your time in politics.
If you want to be a lawyer, politics will ruin your career. You will get into trouble with the authorities, who are often our allies in this work.
You will lose your clients, run out of money, destroy your family, and end up in jail.

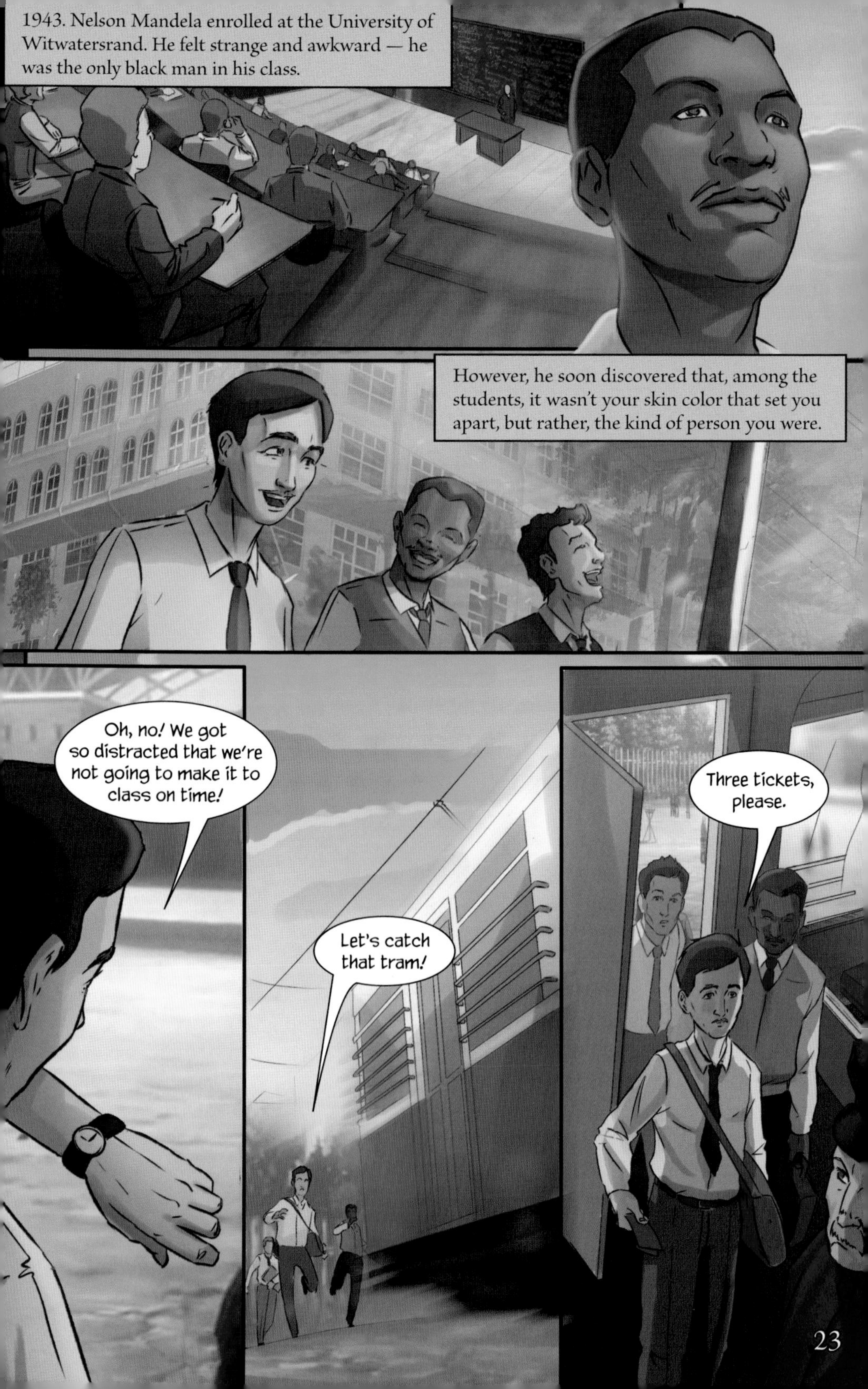
1943. Nelson Mandela enrolled at the University of Witwatersrand. He felt strange and awkward — he was the only black man in his class.
However, he soon discovered that, among the students, it wasn't your skin color that set you apart, but rather, the kind of person you were.
Oh, no! We got so distracted that we're not going to make it to class on time!
Let's catch that tram!
Three tickets, please.

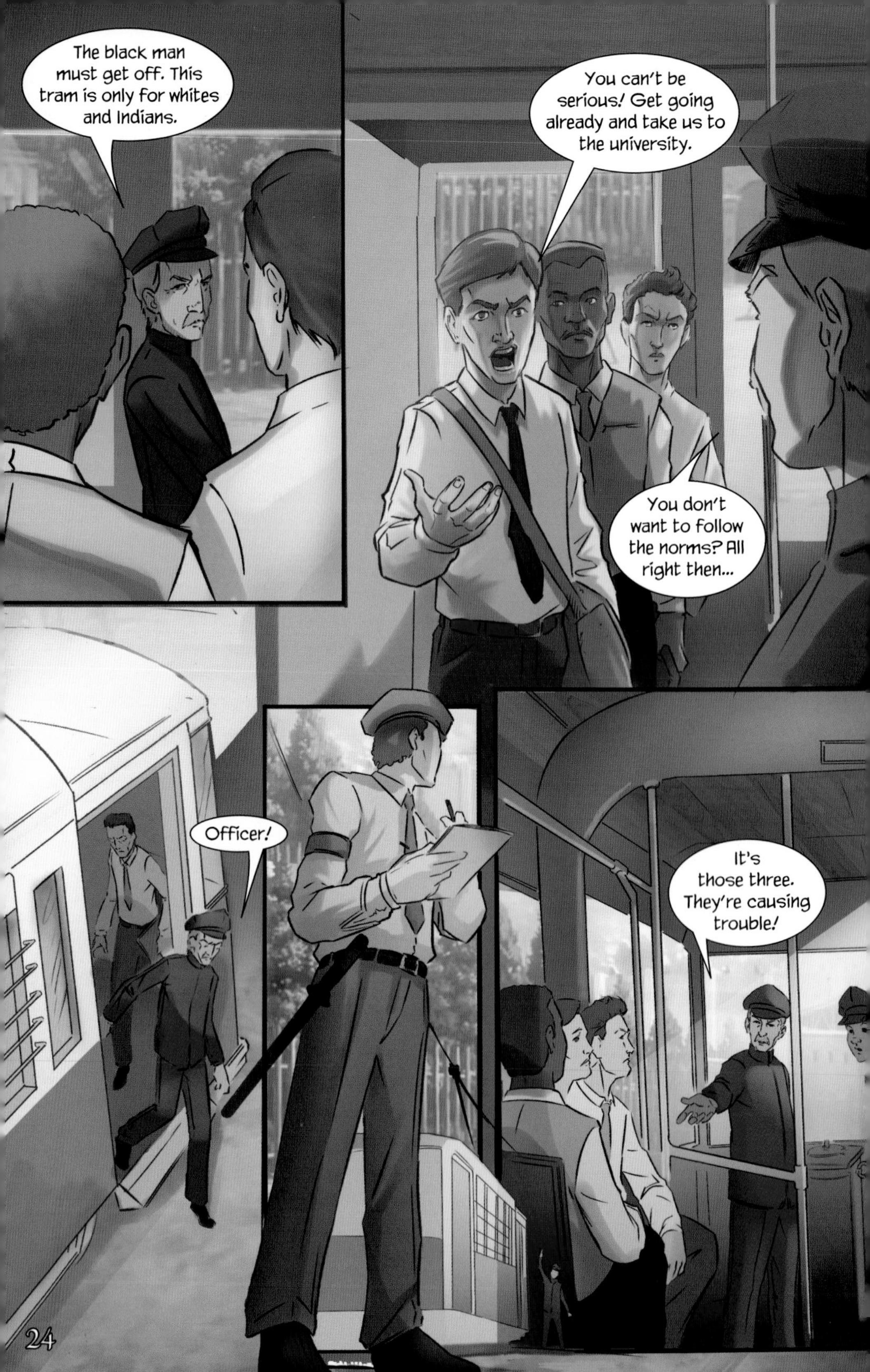
The black man must get off. This tram is only for whites and Indians.
You can't be serious! Get going already and take us to the university.
You don't want to follow the norms? All right then...
Officer!
It's those three. They're causing trouble!

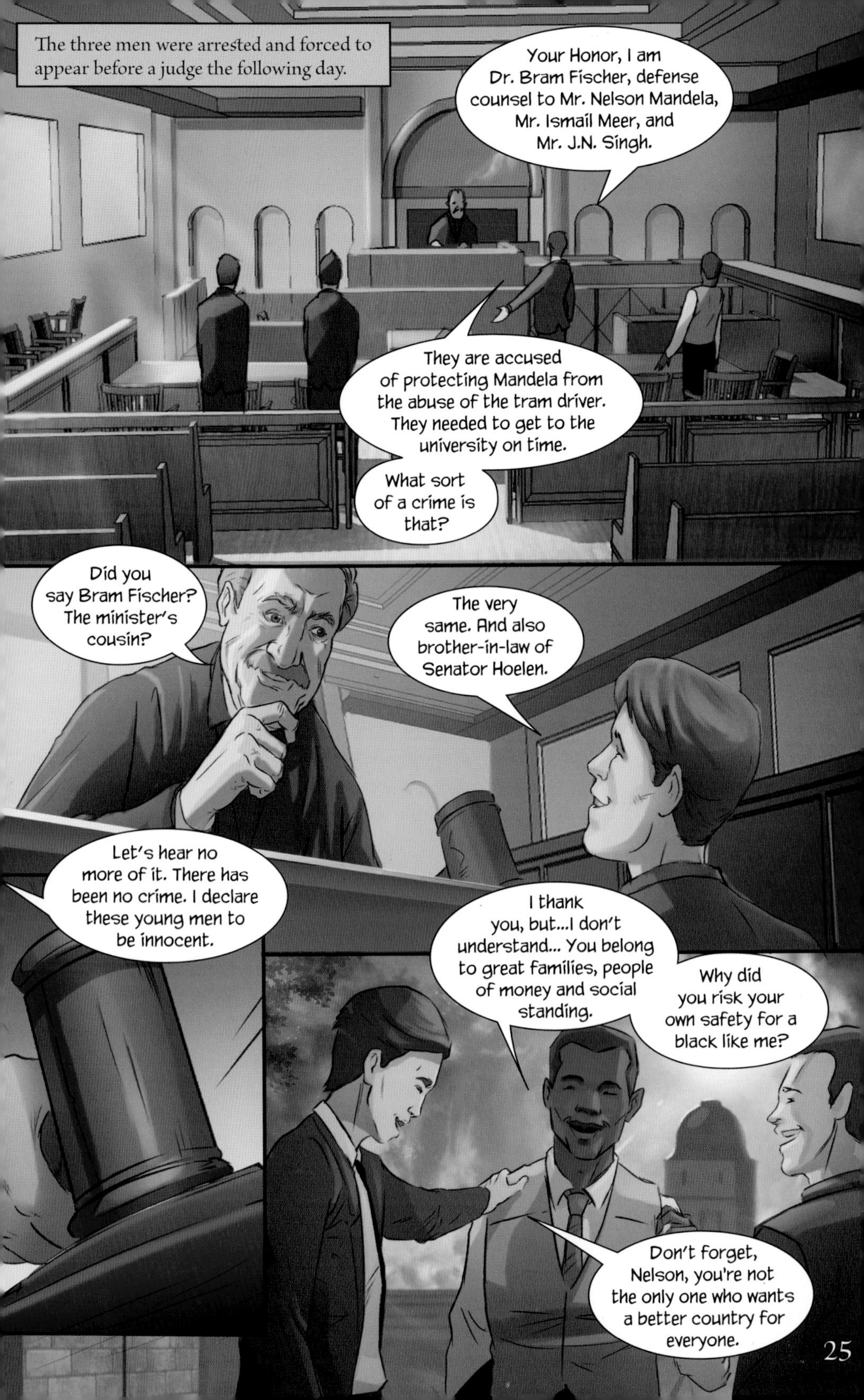
The three men were arrested and forced to appear before a judge the following day.
Your Honor, I am Dr. Bram Fischer, defense counsel to Mr. Nelson Mandela, Mr. Ismail Meer, and Mr. J.N. Singh.
They are accused of protecting Mandela from the abuse of the tram driver. They needed to get to the university on time.
What sort of a crime is that?
Did you say Bram Fischer? The minister's cousin?
The very same. And also brother-in-law of Senator Hoelen.
Let's hear no more of it. There has been no crime. I declare these young men to be innocent.
I thank you, but...I don't understand... You belong to great families, people of money and social standing.
Why did you risk your own safety for a black like me?
Don't forget, Nelson, you're not the only one who wants a better country for everyone.

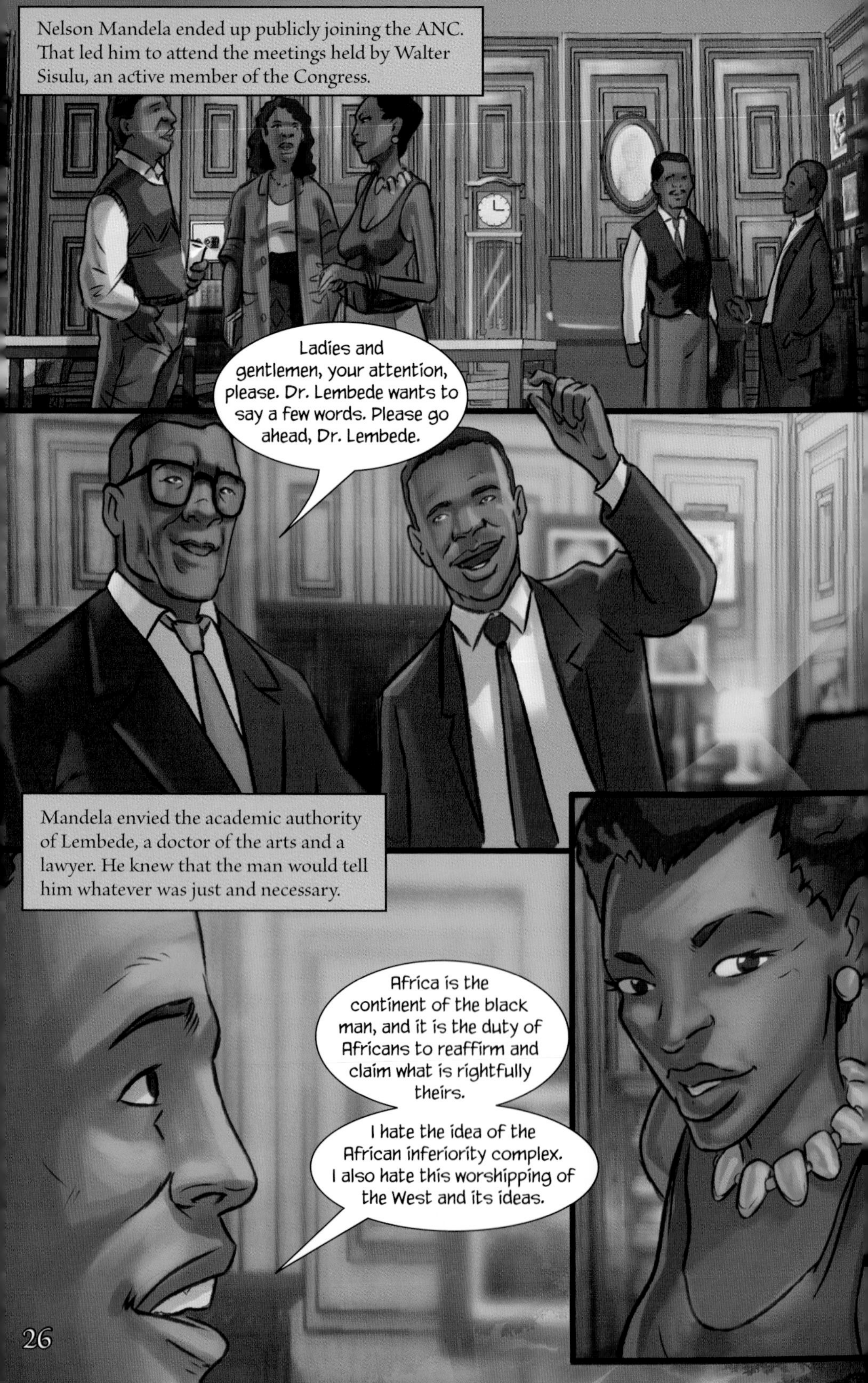
Nelson Mandela ended up publicly joining the ANC. That led him to attend the meetings held by Walter Sisulu, an active member of the Congress.
Ladies and gentlemen, your attention, please. Dr. Lembede wants to say a few words. Please go ahead, Dr. Lembede.
Mandela envied the academic authority of Lembede, a doctor of the arts and a lawyer. He knew that the man would tell him whatever was just and necessary.
Africa is the continent of the black man, and it is the duty of Africans to reaffirm and claim what is rightfully theirs.
I hate the idea of the African inferiority complex. I also hate this worshipping of the West and its ideas.

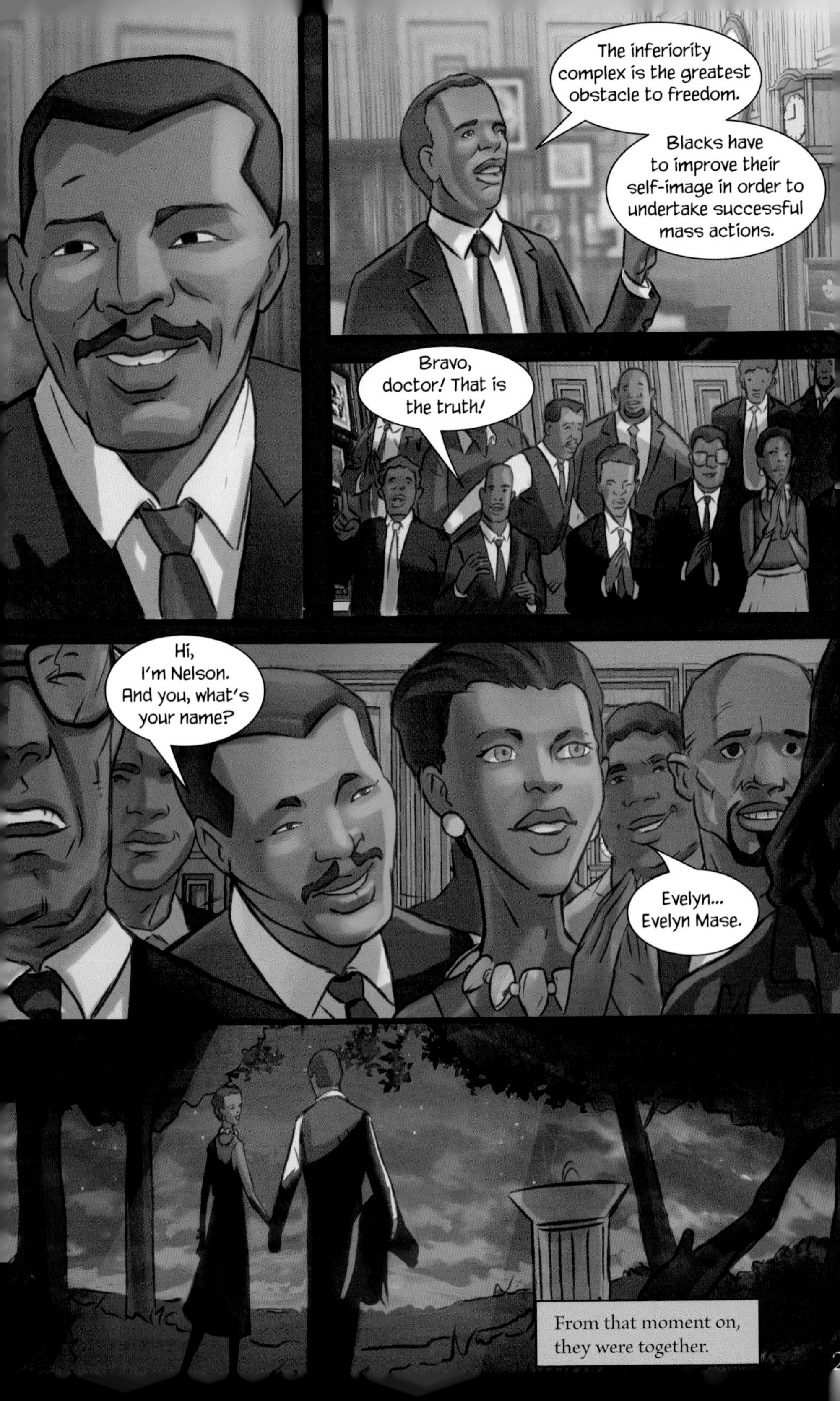
The inferiority complex is the greatest obstacle to freedom.
Blacks have to improve their self-image in order to undertake successful mass actions.
Bravo, doctor! That is the truth!
Hi, I'm Nelson. And you, what's your name?
Evelyn... Evelyn Mase.
From that moment on, they were together.

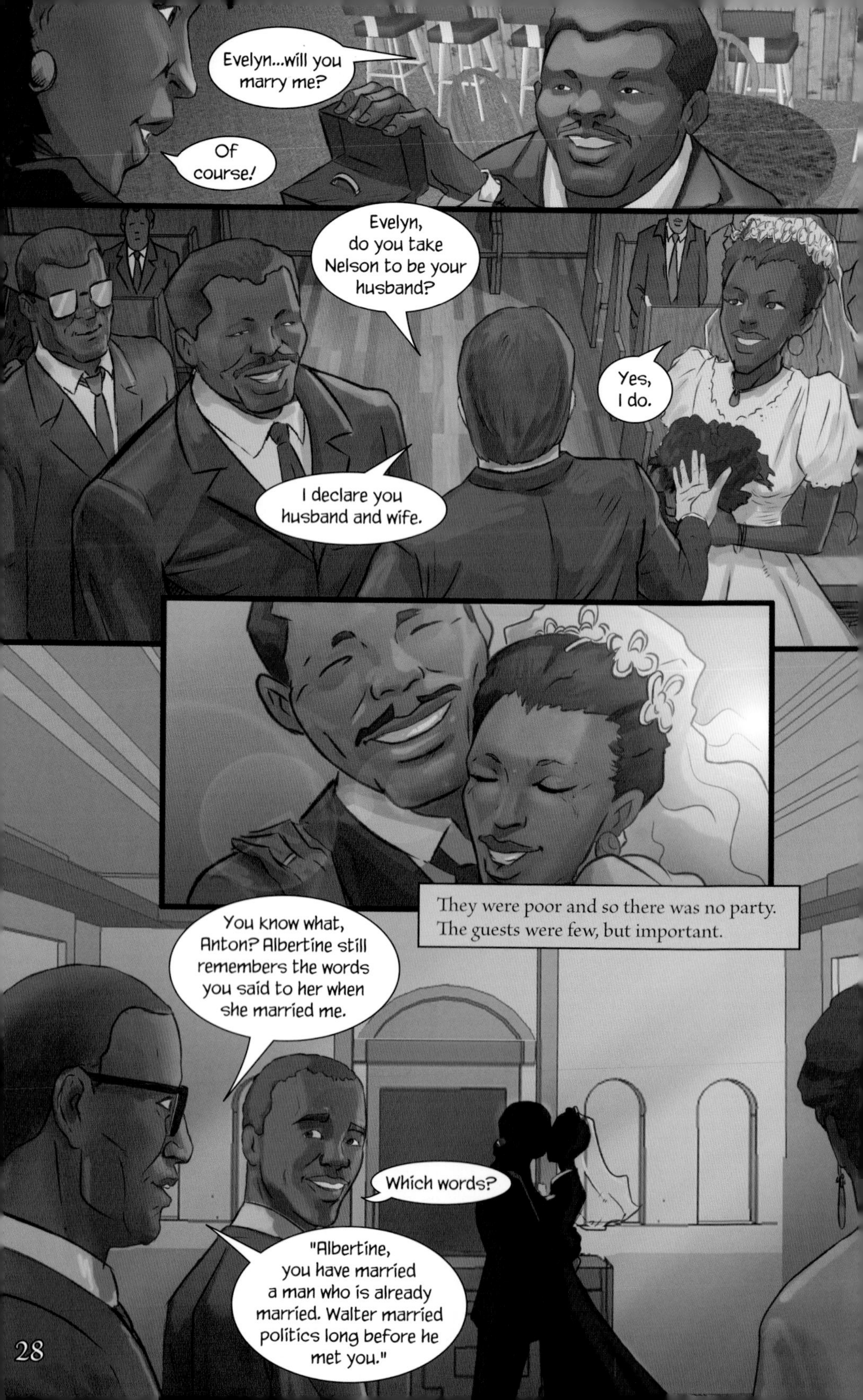
Evelyn...will you marry me?
Of course!
Evelyn, do you take Nelson to be your husband?
Yes, I do.
I declare you husband and wife.
They were poor and so there was no party. The guests were few, but important.
You know what, Anton? Albertine still remembers the words you said to her when she married me.
Which words?
"Albertine, you have married a man who is already married. Walter married politics long before he met you."

CHAPTER 4
JOURNEY TO THE ROOTS

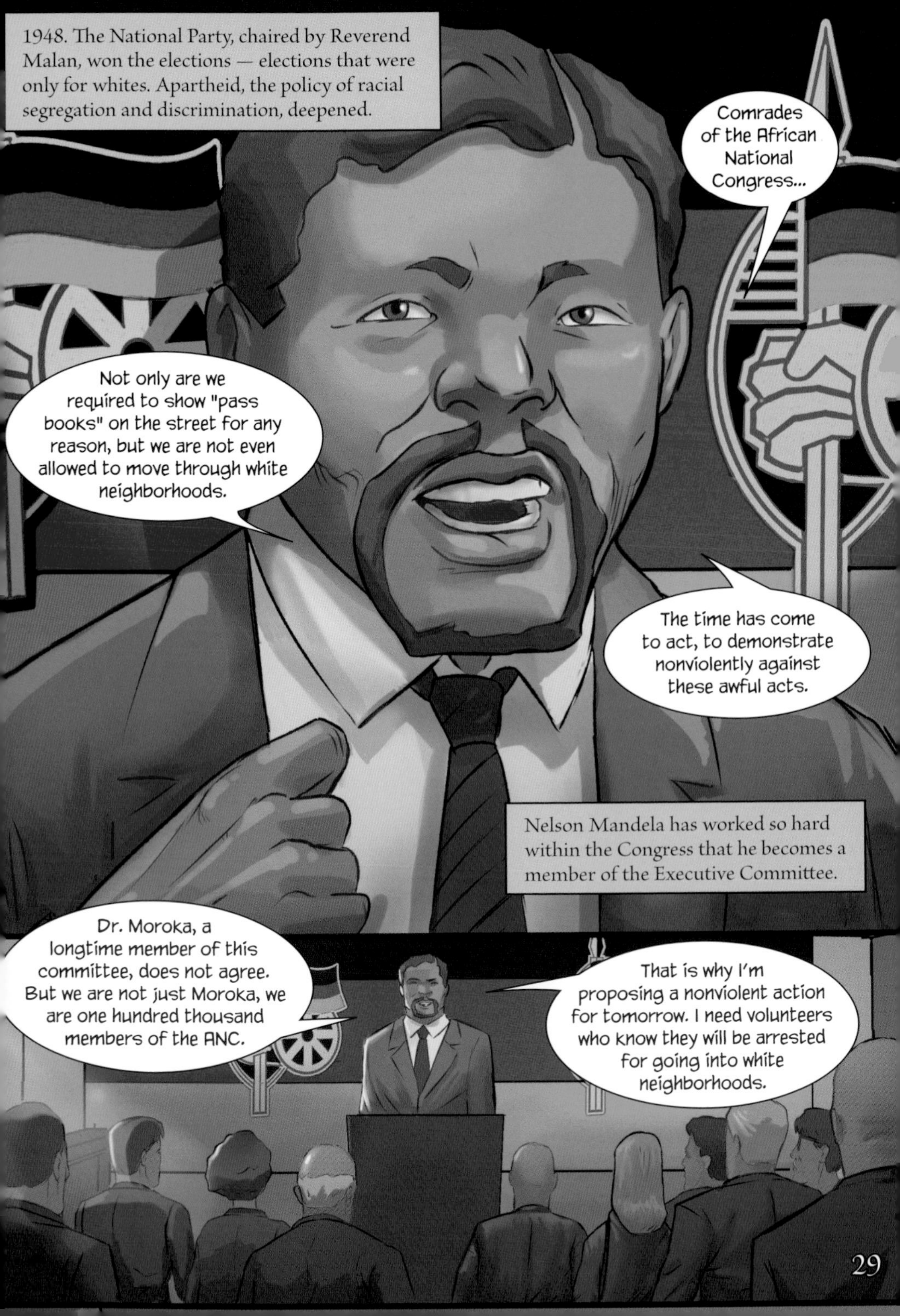
1948. The National Party, chaired by Reverend Malan, won the elections — elections that were only for whites. Apartheid, the policy of racial segregation and discrimination, deepened.
Comrades of the African National Congress...
Not only are we required to show "pass books" on the street for any reason, but we are not even allowed to move through white neighborhoods.
The time has come to act, to demonstrate nonviolently against these awful acts.
Nelson Mandela has worked so hard within the Congress that he becomes a member of the Executive Committee.
Dr. Moroka, a longtime member of this committee, does not agree. But we are not just Moroka, we are one hundred thousand members of the ANC.
That is why I'm proposing a nonviolent action for tomorrow. I need volunteers who know they will be arrested for going into white neighborhoods.

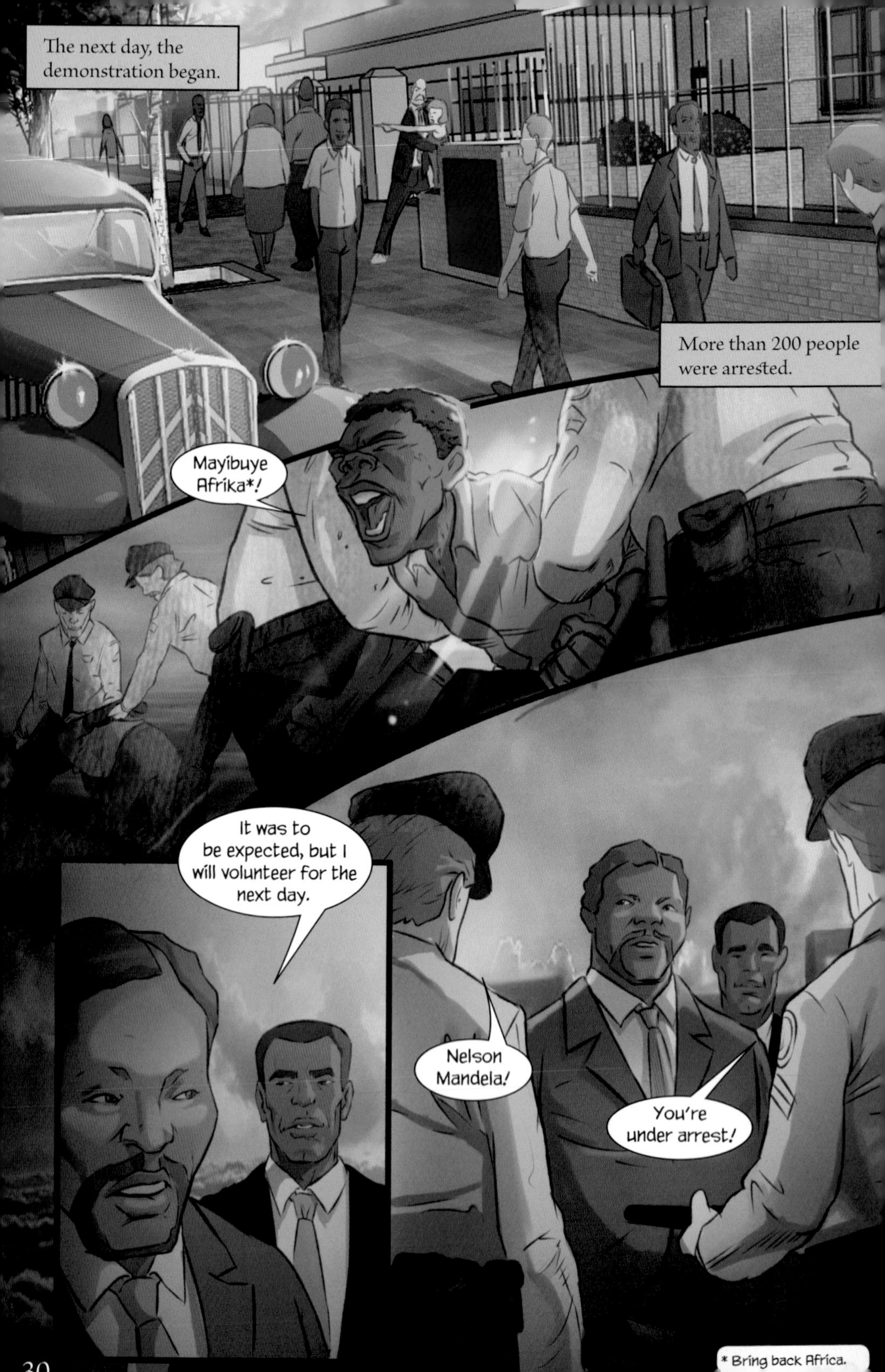

The next day, the demonstration began.
More than 200 people were arrested.
Mayibuye Afrika*!
It was to be expected, but I will volunteer for the next day.
Nelson Mandela!
You're under arrest!
* Bring back Africa.

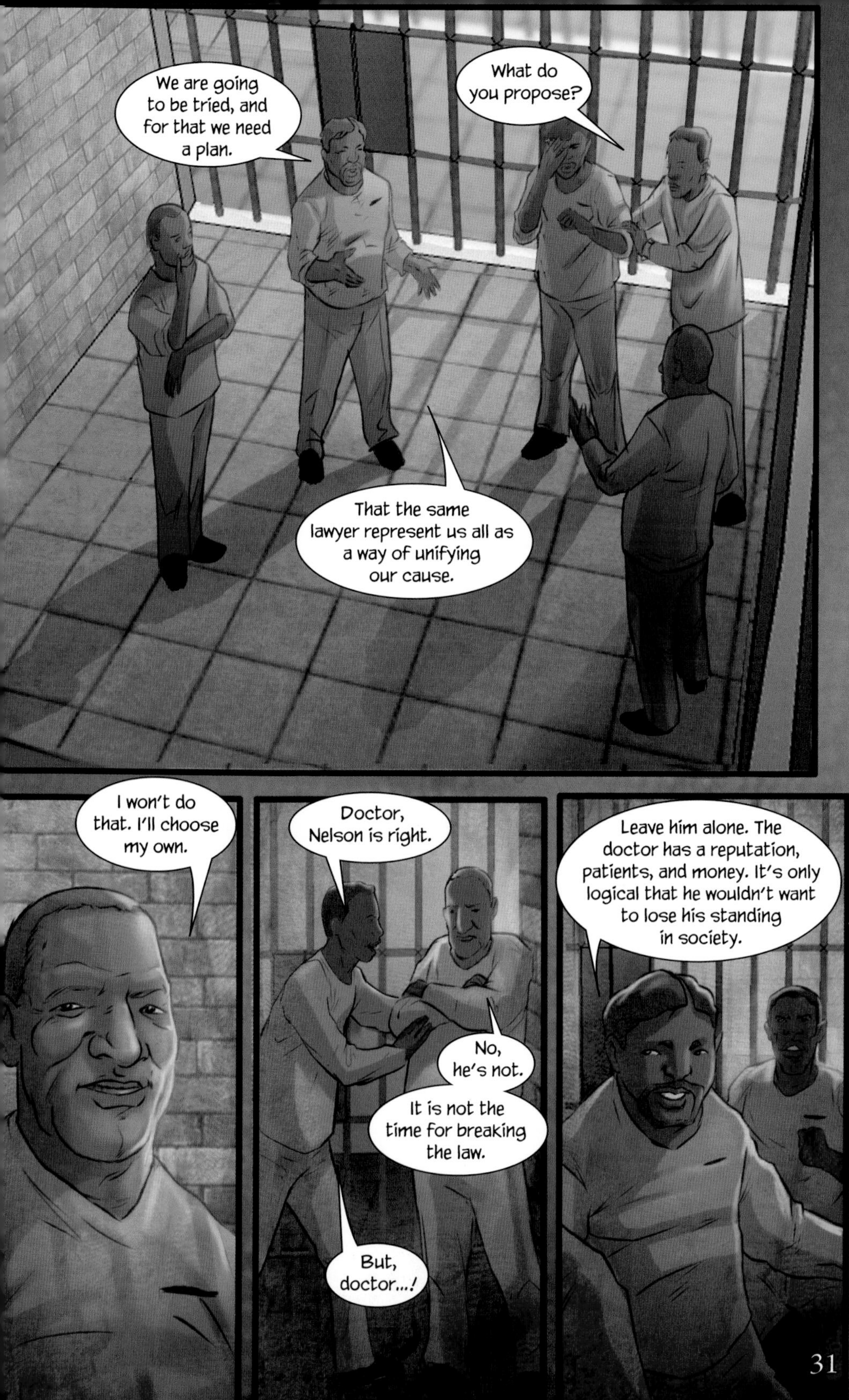
We are going to be tried, and for that we need a plan.
What do you propose?
That the same lawyer represent us all as a way of unifying our cause.
I won't do that. I'll choose my own.
Doctor, Nelson is right.
No, he's not.
It is not the time for breaking the law.
But, doctor...!
Leave him alone. The doctor has a reputation, patients, and money. It's only logical that he wouldn't want to lose his standing in society.

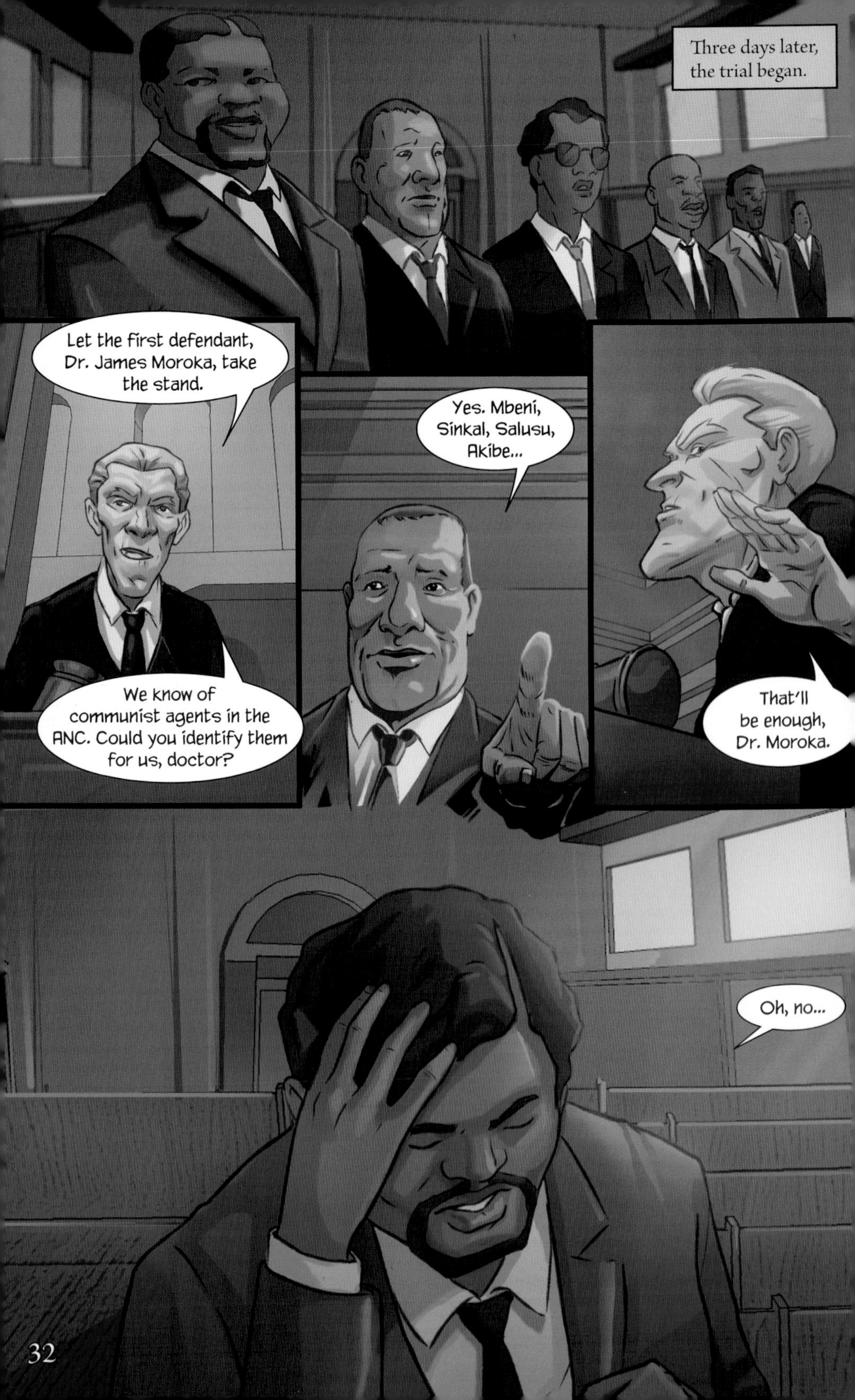

Three days later, the trial began.
Let the first defendant, Dr. James Moroka, take the stand.
We know of communist agents in the ANC. Could you identify them for us, doctor?
Yes. Mbeni, Sinkal, Salusu, Akibe...
That'll be enough, Dr. Moroka.
Oh, no...

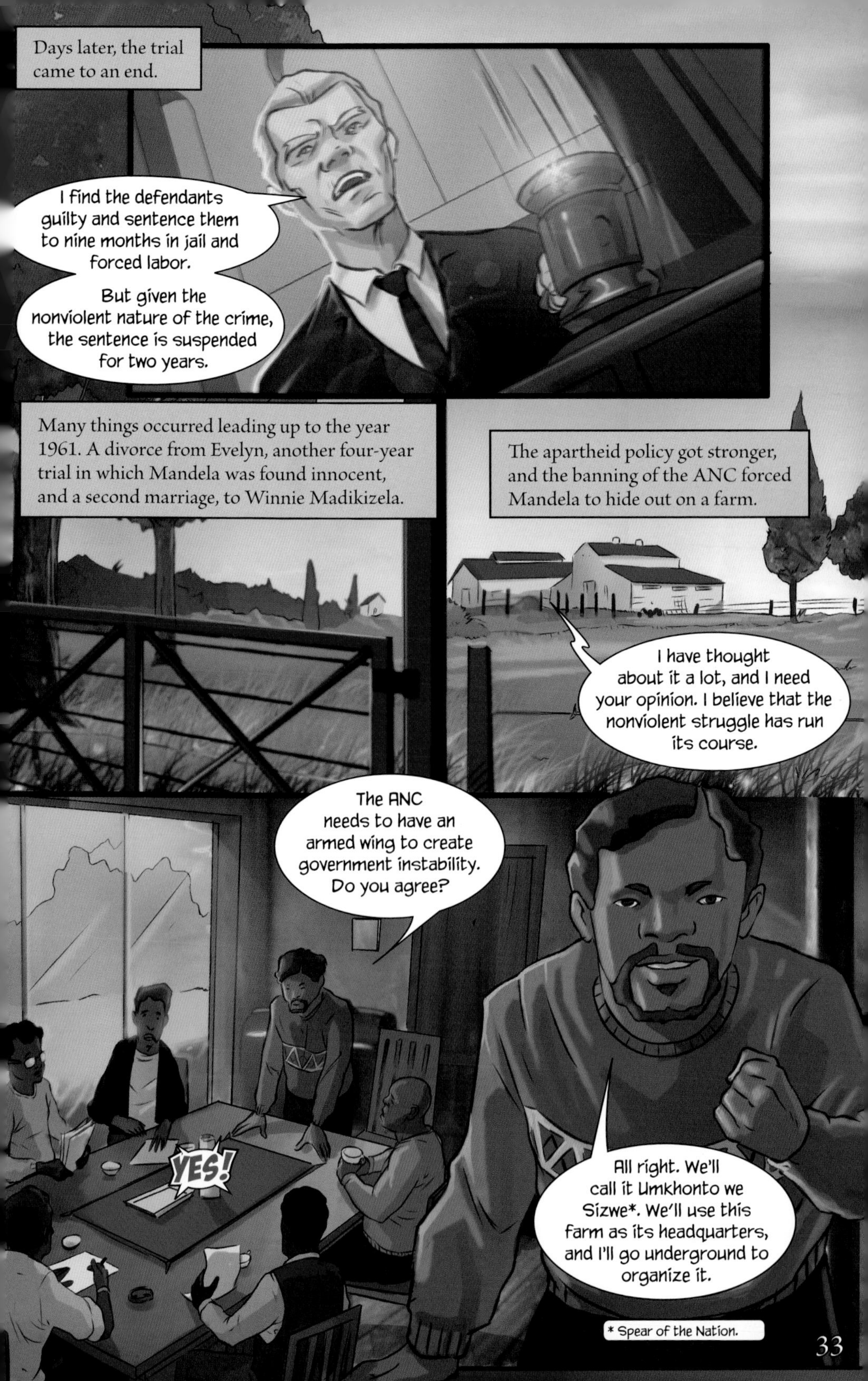
Days later, the trial came to an end.
I find the defendants guilty and sentence them to nine months in jail and forced labor.
But given the nonviolent nature of the crime, the sentence is suspended for two years.
Many things occurred leading up to the year 1961. A divorce from Evelyn, another four-year trial in which Mandela was found innocent, and a second marriage, to Winnie Madikizela.
The apartheid policy got stronger, and the banning of the ANC forced Mandela to hide out on a farm.
I have thought about it a lot, and I need your opinion. I believe that the nonviolent struggle has run its course.
The ANC needs to have an armed wing to create government instability. Do you agree?
YES!
All right. We'll call it Umkhonto we Sizwe*. We'll use this farm as its headquarters, and I'll go underground to organize it.
* Spear of the Nation.

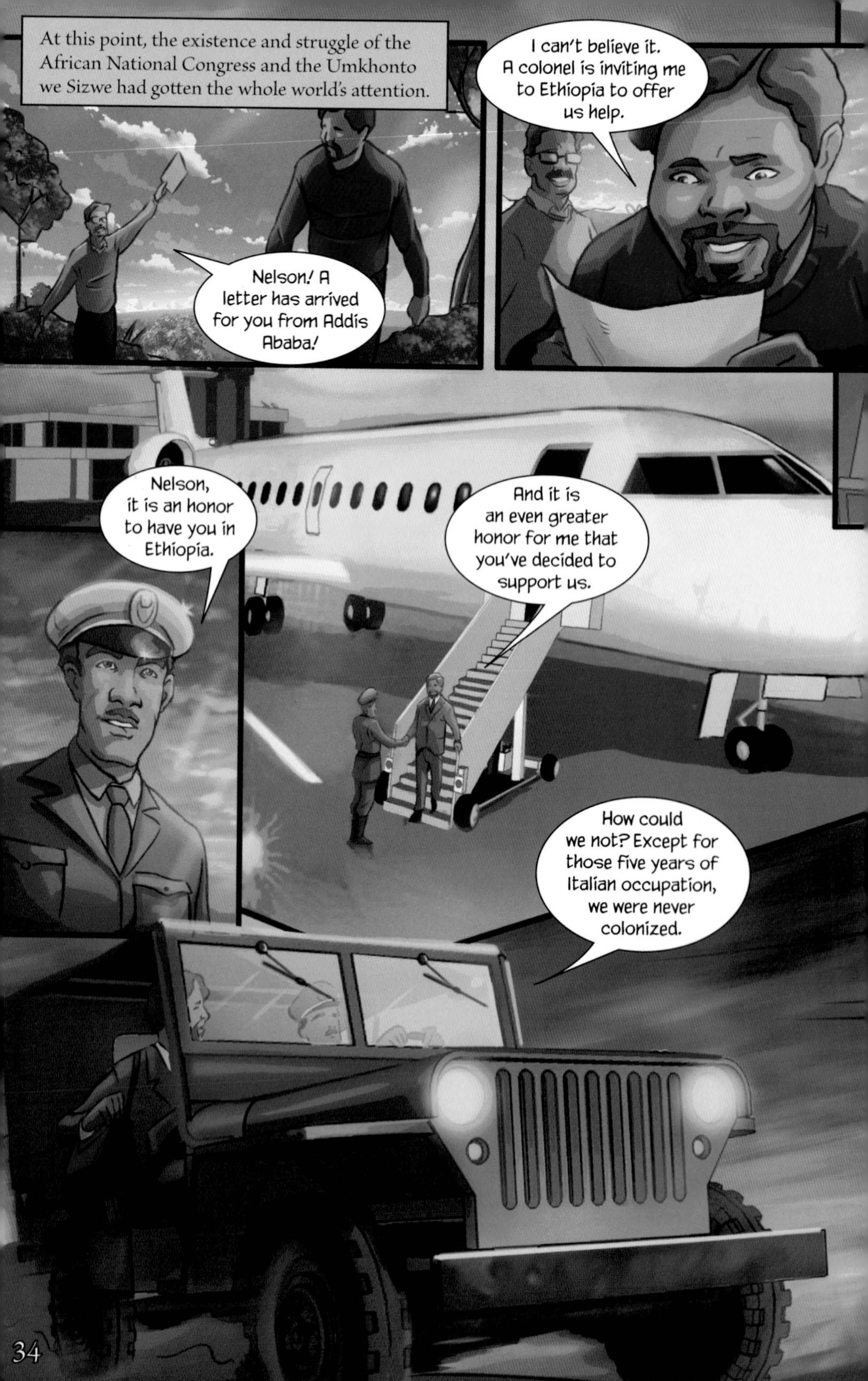
At this point, the existence and struggle of the African National Congress and the Umkhonto we Sizwe had gotten the whole world's attention.
Nelson! A letter has arrived for you from Addis Ababa!
I can't believe it. A colonel is inviting me to Ethiopia to offer us help.
Nelson, it is an honor to have you in Ethiopia.
And it is an even greater honor for me that you've decided to support us.
How could we not? Except for those five years of Italian occupation, we were never colonized.

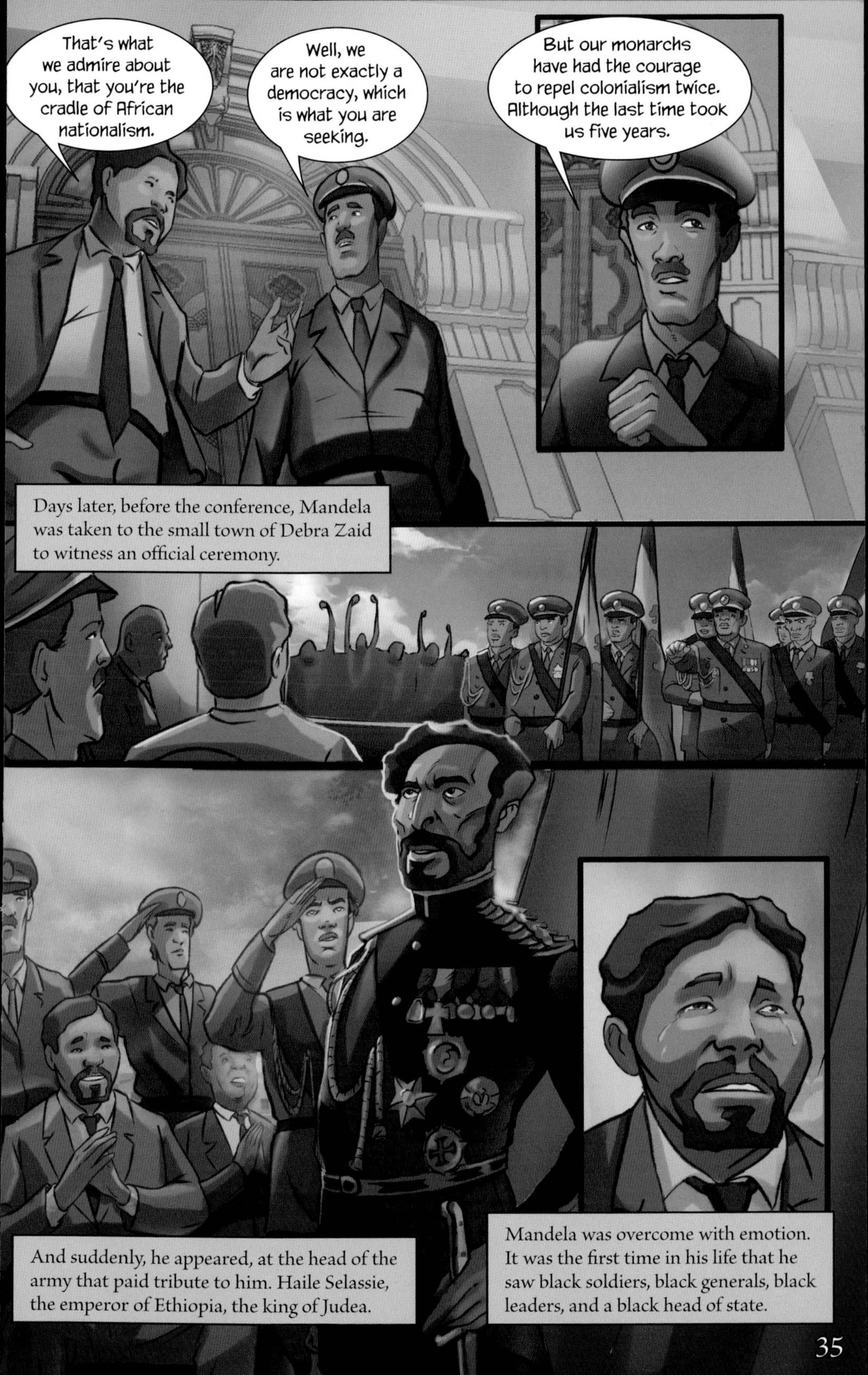
That's what we admire about you, that you're the cradle of African nationalism.
Well, we are not exactly a democracy, which is what you are seeking.
But our monarchs have had the courage to repel colonialism twice. Although the last time took us five years.
Days later, before the conference, Mandela was taken to the small town of Debra Zaid to witness an official ceremony.
And suddenly, he appeared, at the head of the army that paid tribute to him. Haile Selassie, the emperor of Ethiopia, the king of Judea.
Mandela was overcome with emotion. It was the first time in his life that he saw black soldiers, black generals, black leaders, and a black head of state.

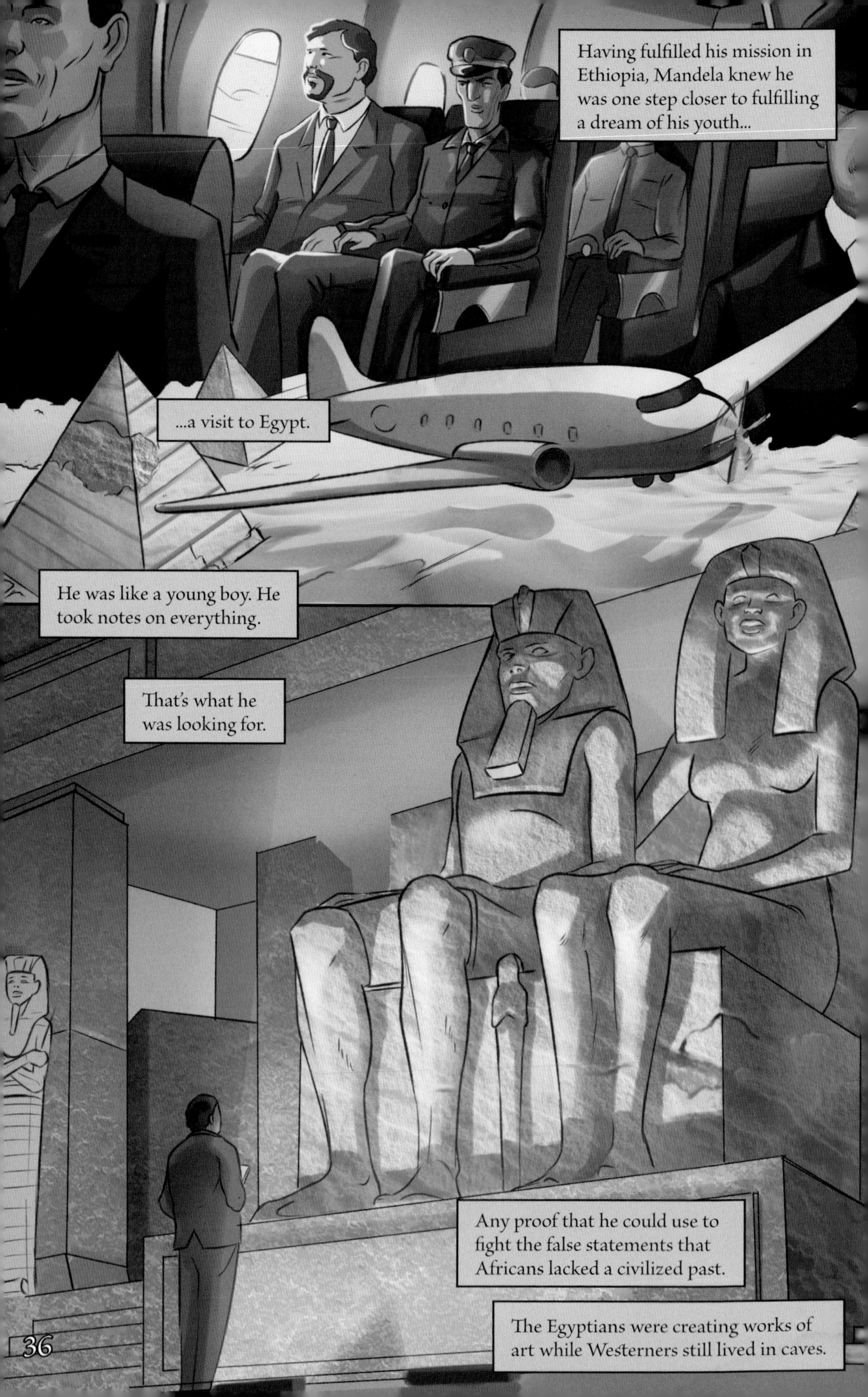
Having fulfilled his mission in Ethiopia, Mandela knew he was one step closer to fulfilling a dream of his youth...
...a visit to Egypt.
He was like a young boy. He took notes on everything.
That's what he was looking for.
Any proof that he could use to fight the false statements that Africans lacked a civilized past.
The Egyptians were creating works of art while Westerners still lived in caves.

CHAPTER 5
ROBBEN ISLAND

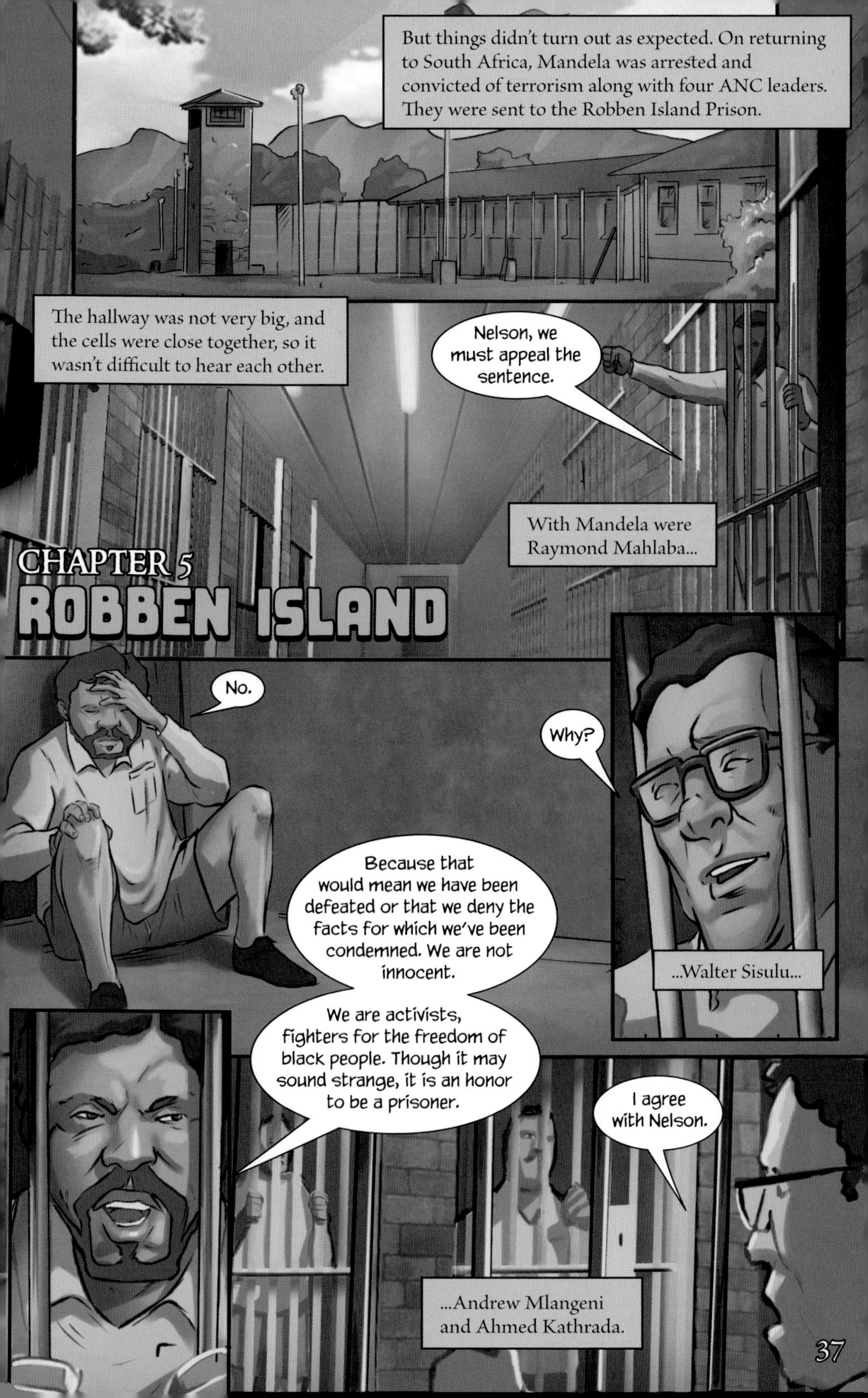
But things didn't turn out as expected. On returning to South Africa, Mandela was arrested and convicted of terrorism along with four ANC leaders. They were sent to the Robben Island Prison.
The hallway was not very big, and the cells were close together, so it wasn't difficult to hear each other.
Nelson, we must appeal the sentence.
With Mandela were Raymond Mahlaba...
No.
Why?
...Walter Sisulu...
Because that would mean we have been defeated or that we deny the facts for which we've been condemned. We are not innocent.
We are activists, fighters for the freedom of black people. Though it may sound strange, it is an honor to be a prisoner.
I agree with Nelson.
...Andrew Mlangeni and Ahmed Kathrada.

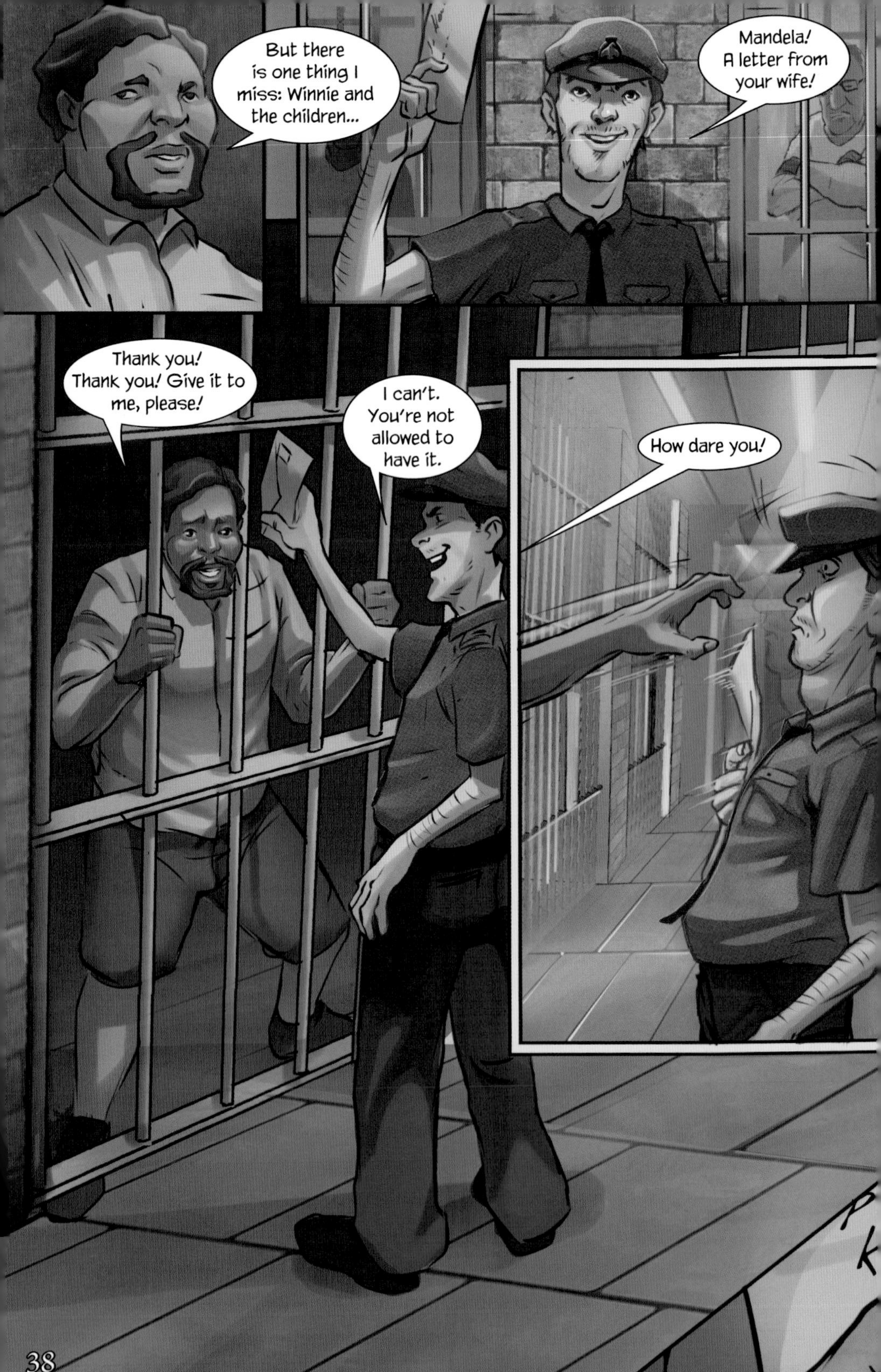
But there is one thing I miss: Winnie and the children...
Mandela! A letter from your wife!
Thank you! Thank you! Give it to me, please!
I can't. You're not allowed to have it.
How dare you!

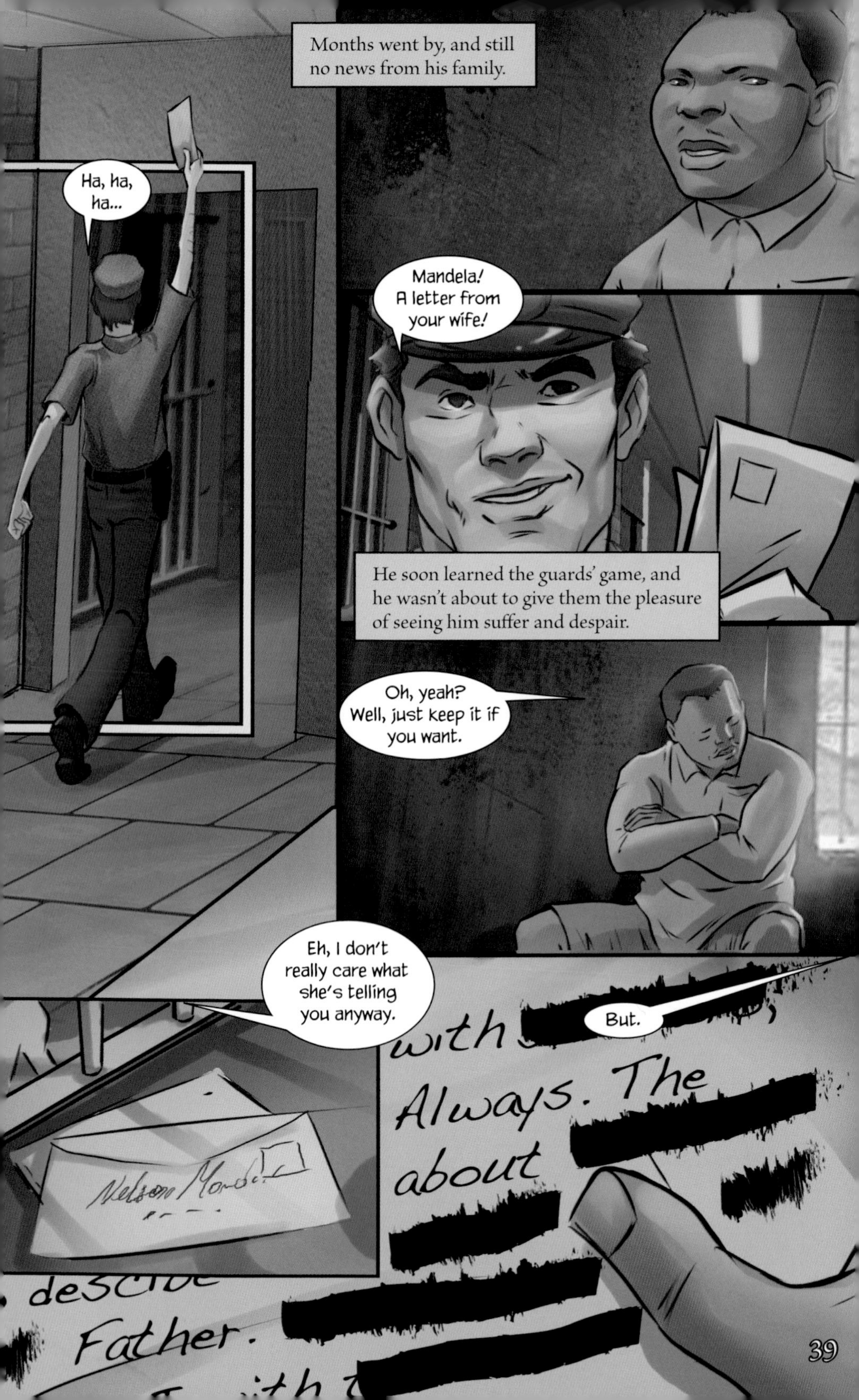
Months went by, and still no news from his family.
Ha, ha, ha...
Mandela! A letter from your wife!
He soon learned the guards' game, and he wasn't about to give them the pleasure of seeing him suffer and despair.
Oh, yeah? Well, just keep it if you want.
Eh, I don't really care what she's telling you anyway.
But.
with [redacted]
Always. The [redacted]
about [redacted]
Father. [redacted]

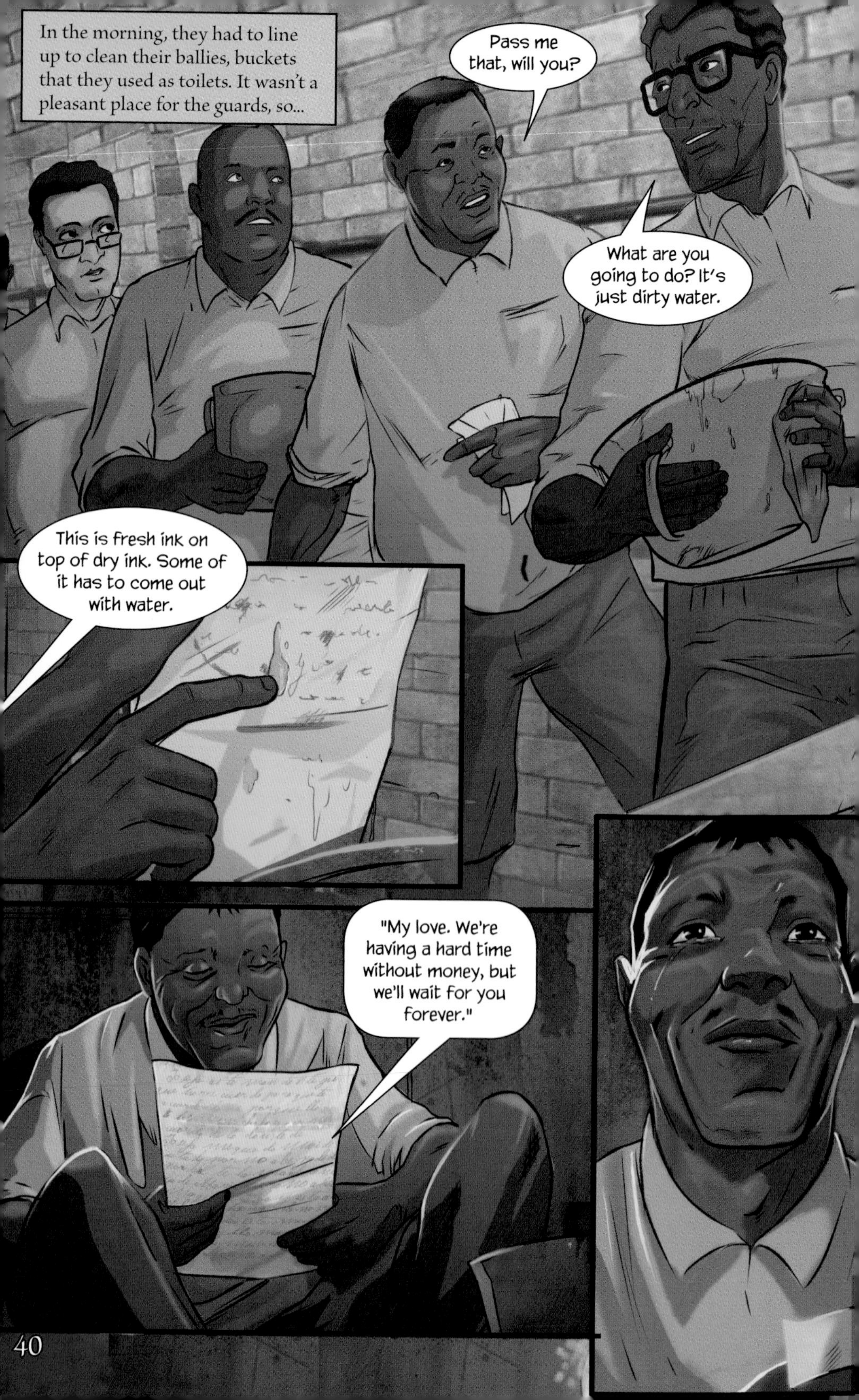
In the morning, they had to line up to clean their ballies, buckets that they used as toilets. It wasn't a pleasant place for the guards, so...
Pass me that, will you?
What are you going to do? It's just dirty water.
This is fresh ink on top of dry ink. Some of it has to come out with water.
"My love. We're having a hard time without money, but we'll wait for you forever."

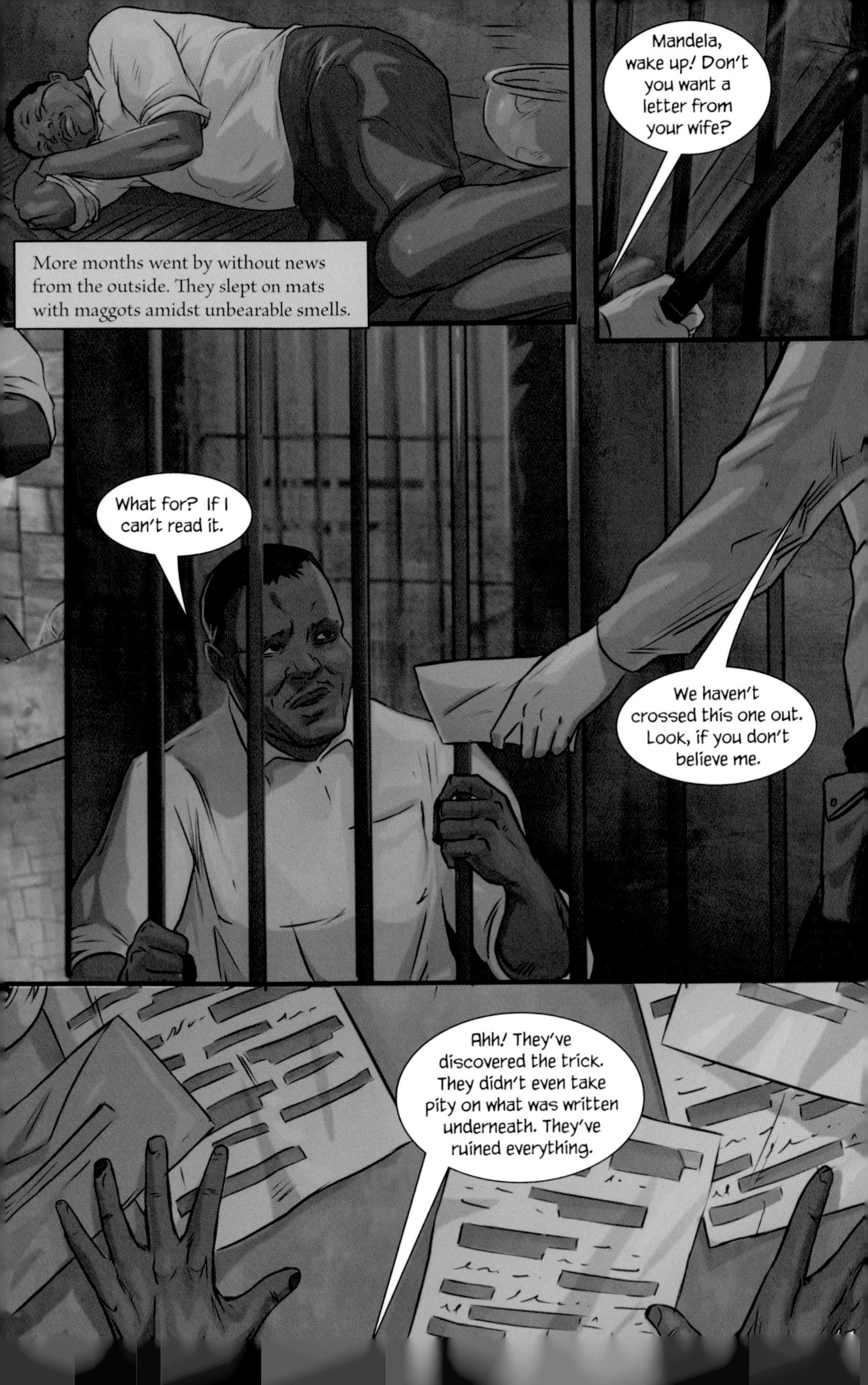
More months went by without news from the outside. They slept on mats with maggots amidst unbearable smells.
Mandela, wake up! Don't you want a letter from your wife?
What for? If I can't read it.
We haven't crossed this one out. Look, if you don't believe me.
Ahh! They've discovered the trick. They didn't even take pity on what was written underneath. They've ruined everything.

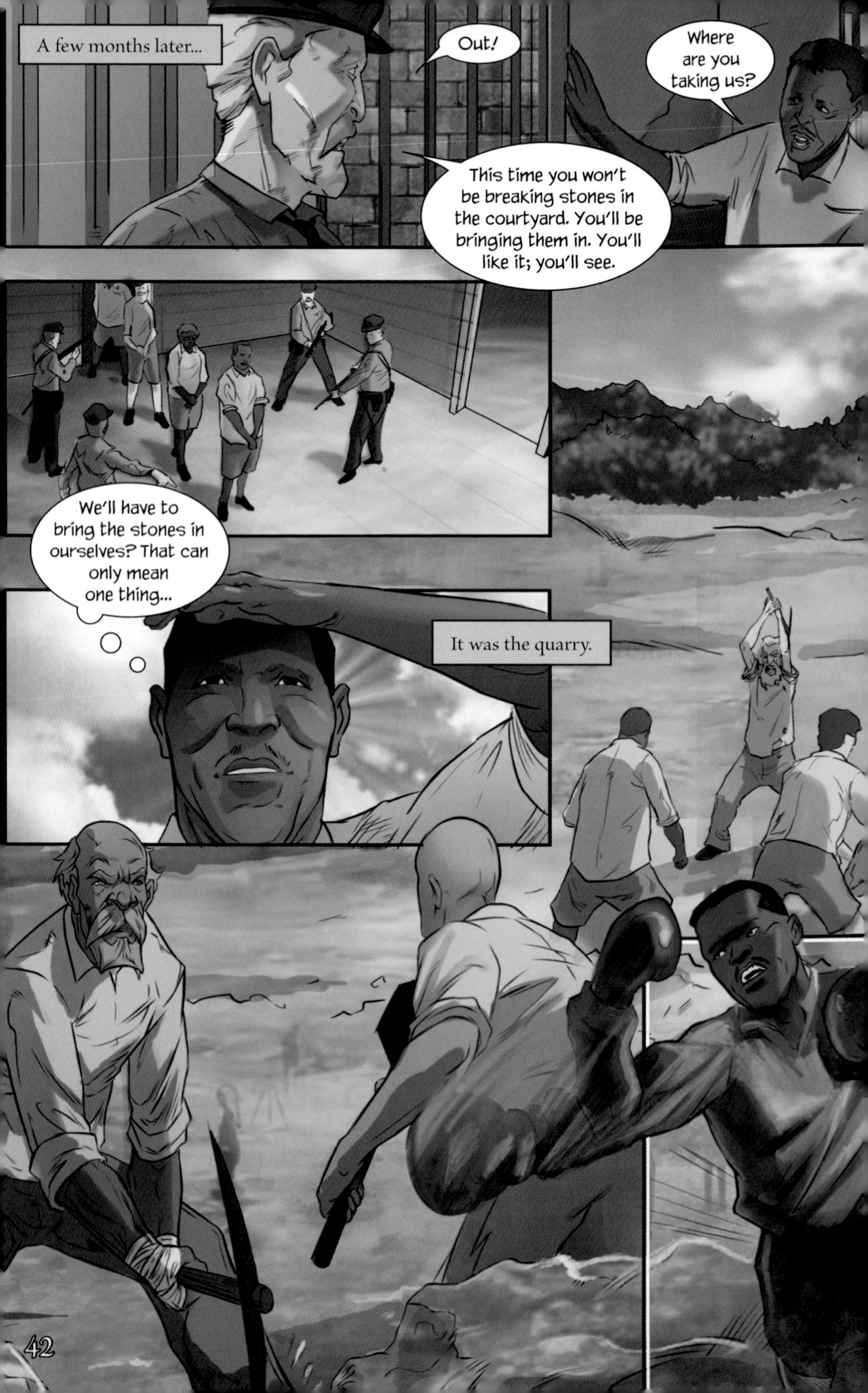
A few months later...
Out!
Where are you taking us?
This time you won't be breaking stones in the courtyard. You'll be bringing them in. You'll like it; you'll see.
We'll have to bring the stones in ourselves? That can only mean one thing...
It was the quarry.

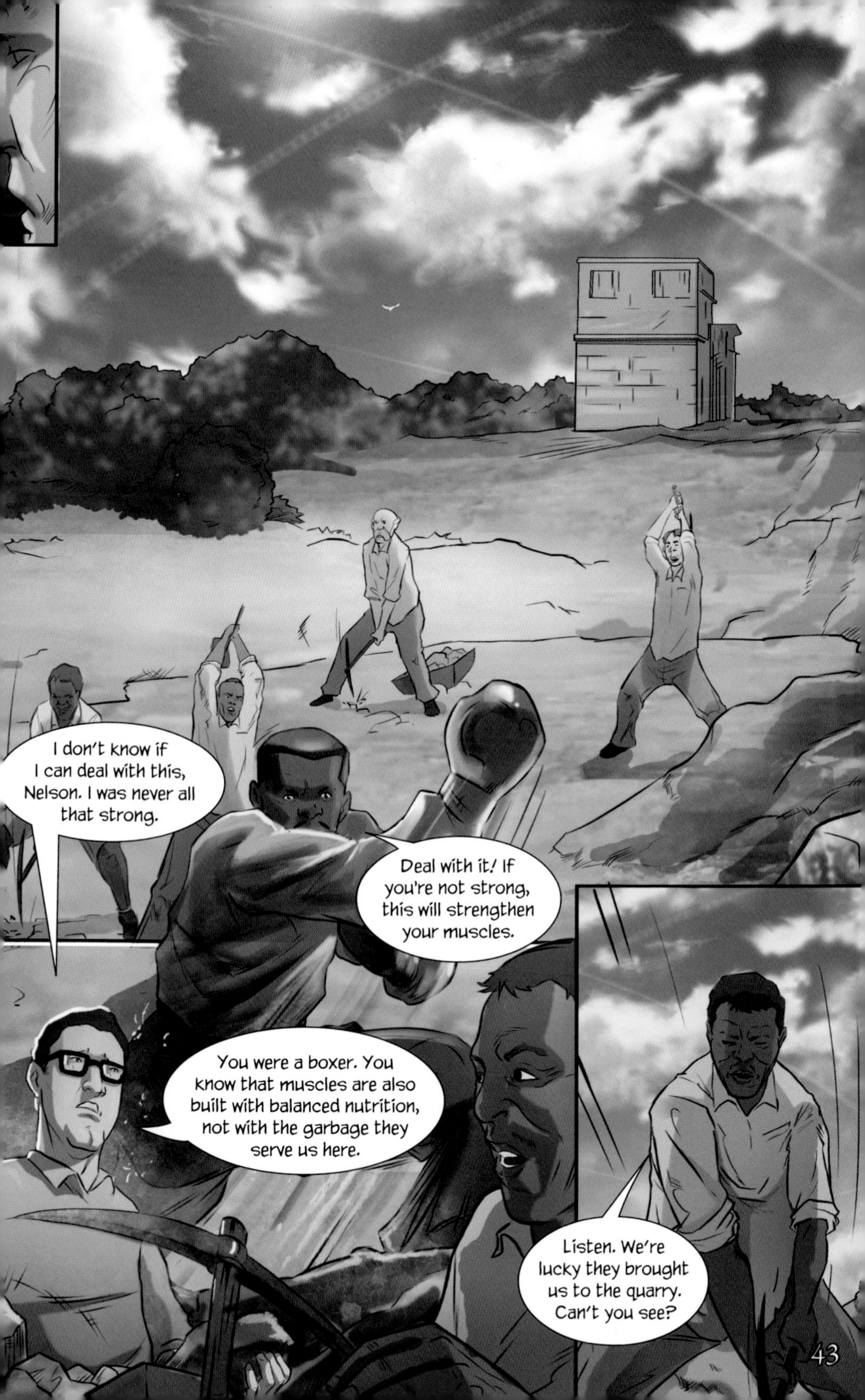
I don't know if I can deal with this, Nelson. I was never all that strong.
Deal with it! If you're not strong, this will strengthen your muscles.
You were a boxer. You know that muscles are also built with balanced nutrition, not with the garbage they serve us here.
Listen. We're lucky they brought us to the quarry. Can't you see?

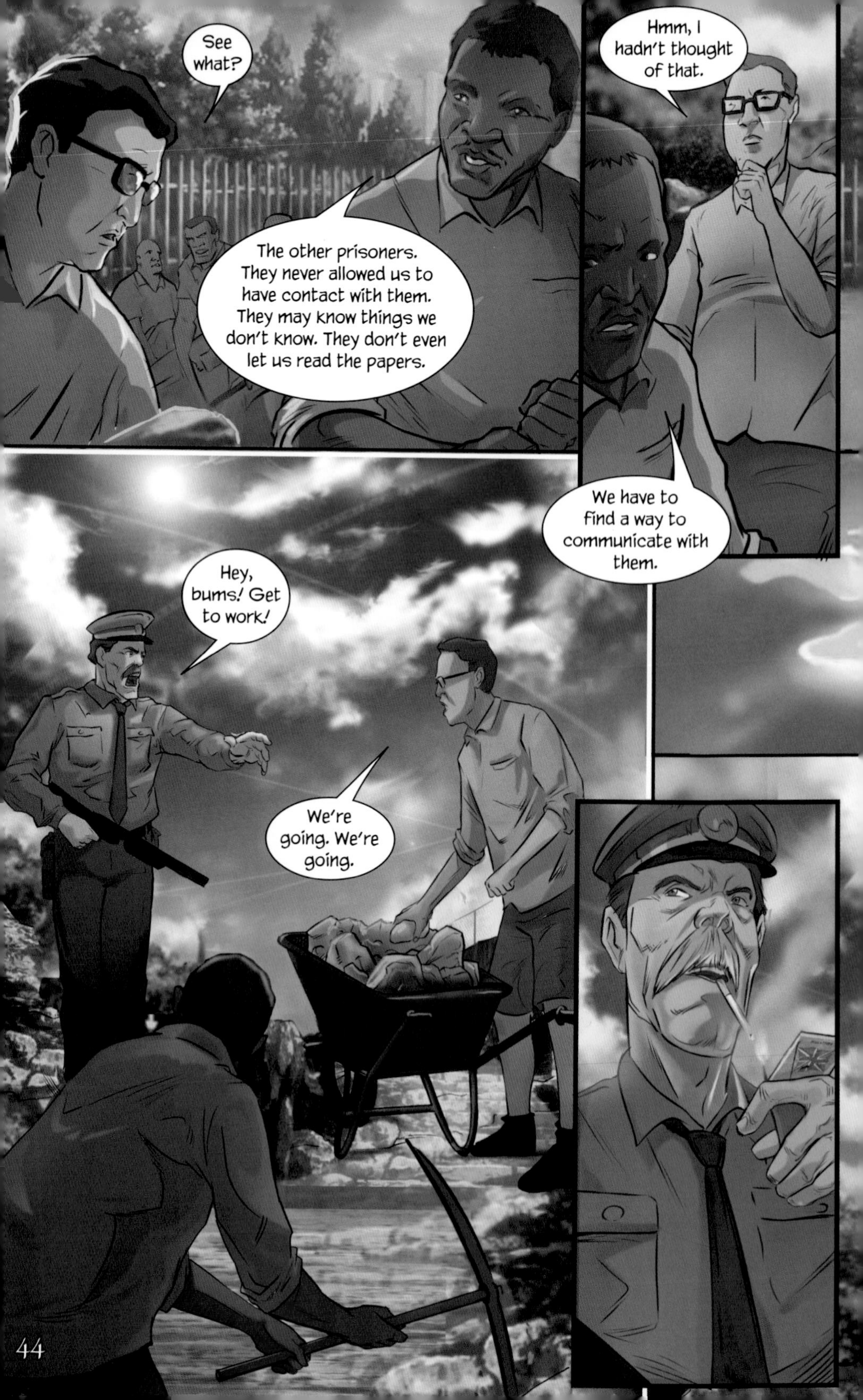
See what?
The other prisoners. They never allowed us to have contact with them. They may know things we don't know. They don't even let us read the papers.
Hmm, I hadn't thought of that.
We have to find a way to communicate with them.
Hey, bums! Get to work!
We're going. We're going.

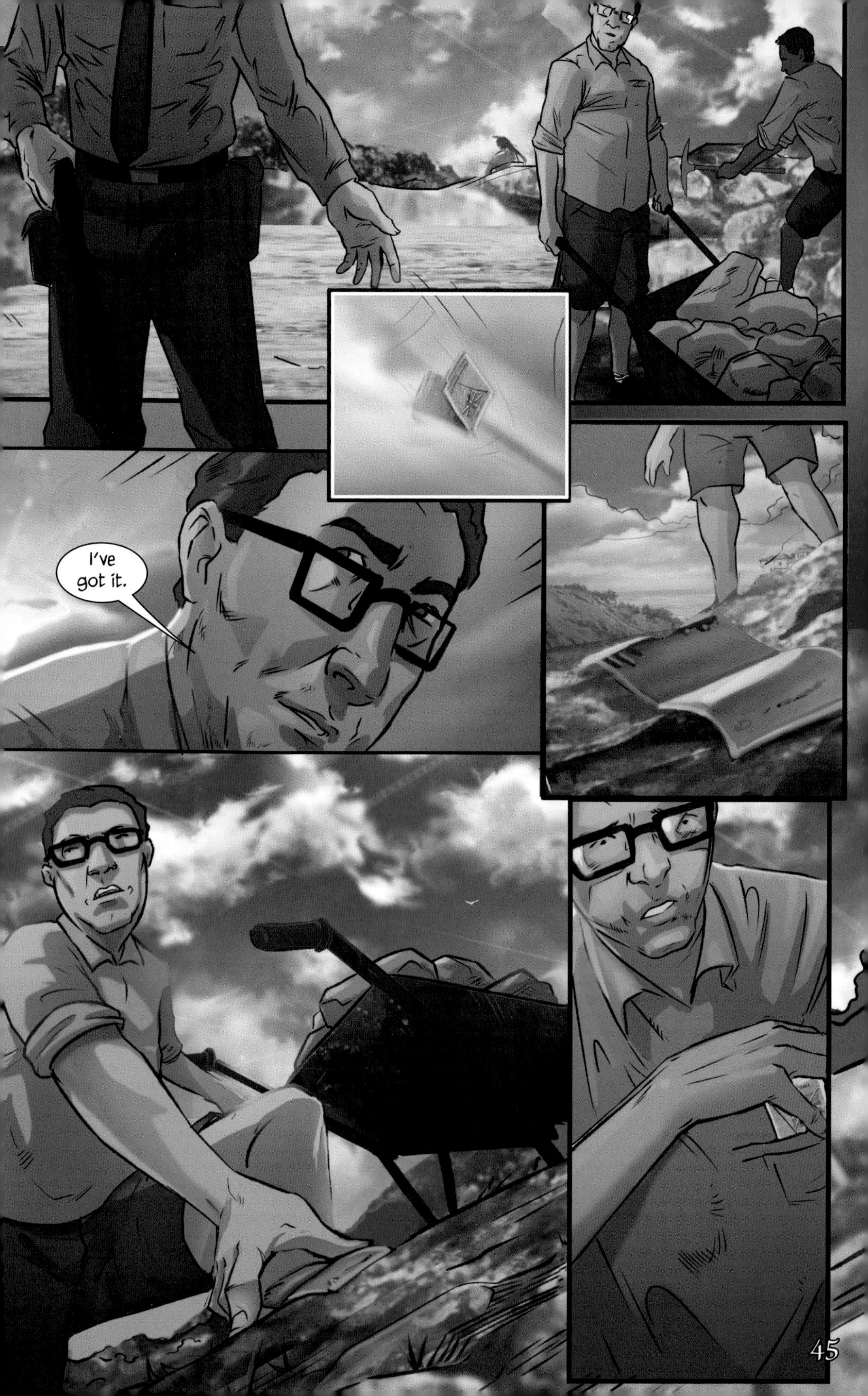
I've got it.

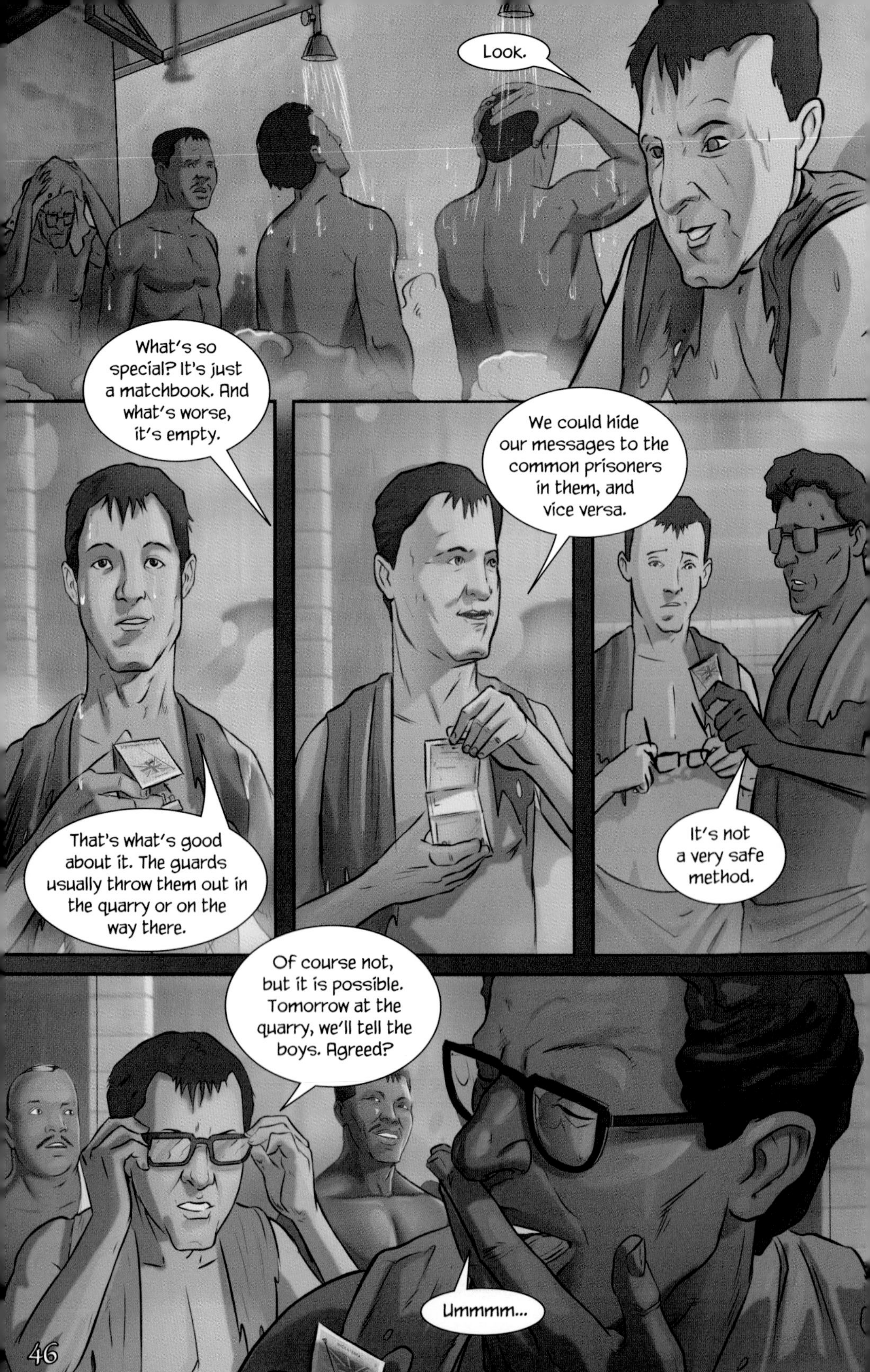

Look.
What's so special? It's just a matchbook. And what's worse, it's empty.
That's what's good about it. The guards usually throw them out in the quarry or on the way there.
We could hide our messages to the common prisoners in them, and vice versa.
It's not a very safe method.
Of course not, but it is possible. Tomorrow at the quarry, we'll tell the boys. Agreed?
Ummmm...

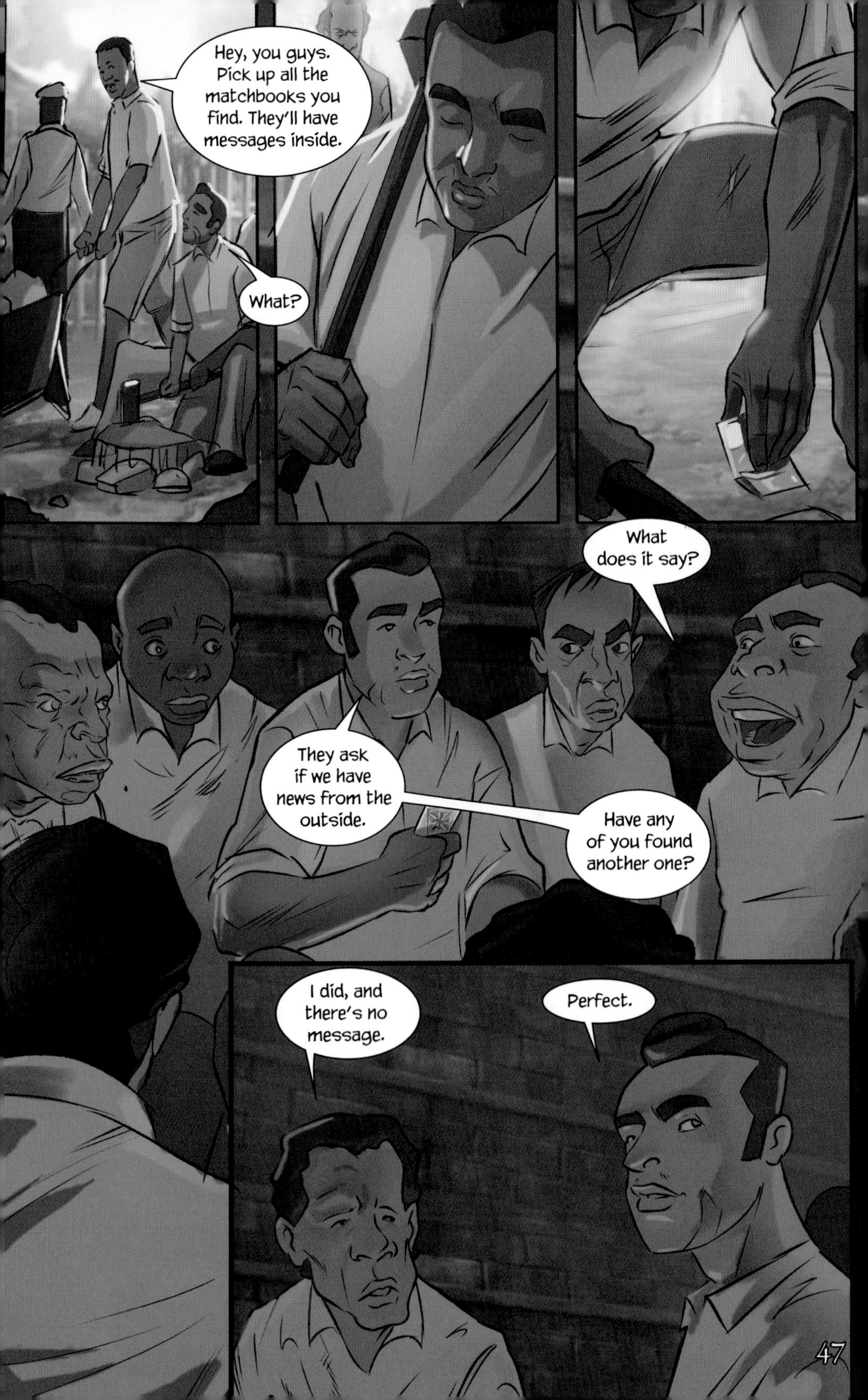
Hey, you guys. Pick up all the matchbooks you find. They'll have messages inside.
What?
What does it say?
They ask if we have news from the outside.
Have any of you found another one?
I did, and there's no message.
Perfect.

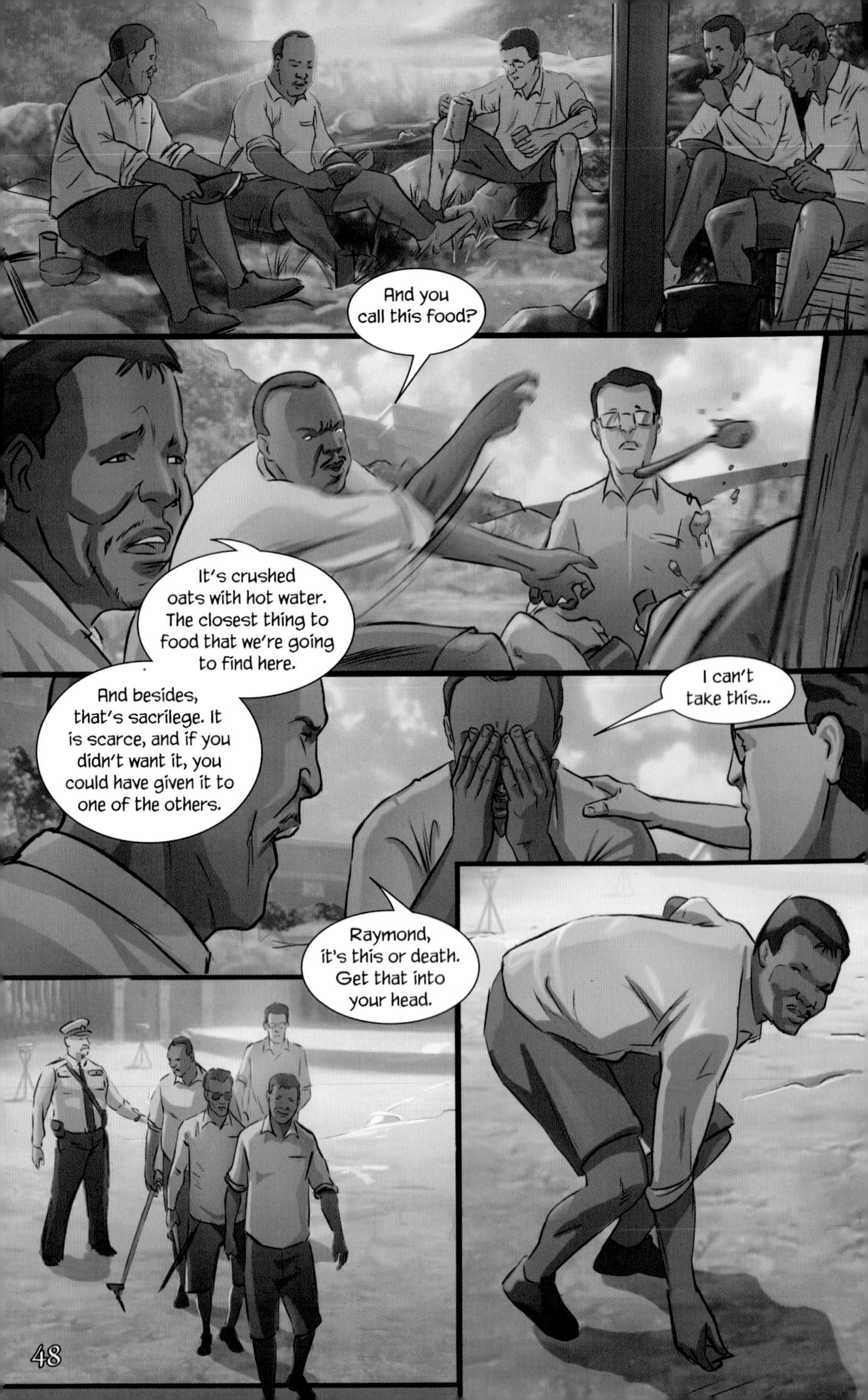
And you call this food?
It's crushed oats with hot water. The closest thing to food that we're going to find here.
And besides, that's sacrilege. It is scarce, and if you didn't want it, you could have given it to one of the others.
I can't take this...
Raymond, it's this or death. Get that into your head.

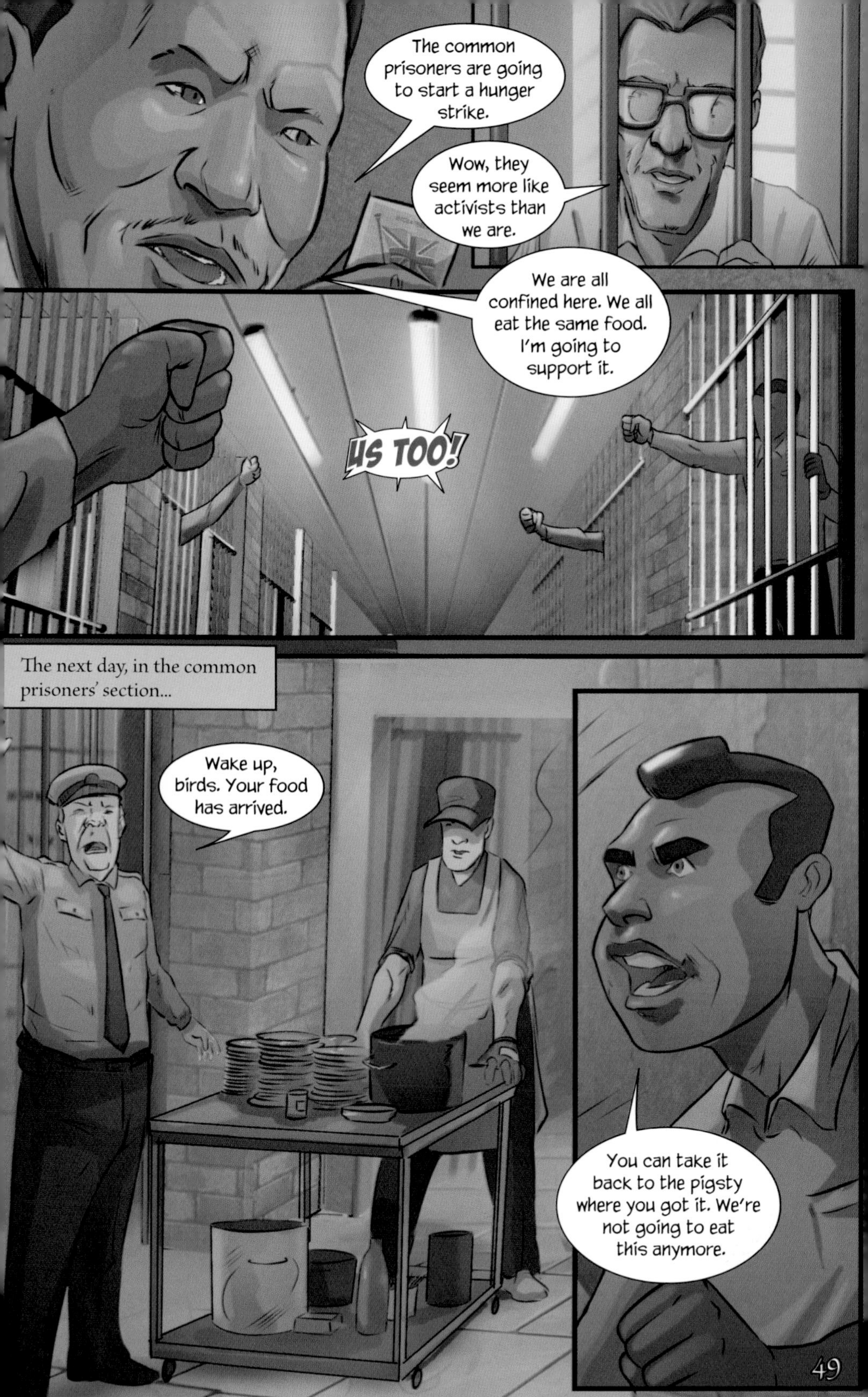
The common prisoners are going to start a hunger strike.
Wow, they seem more like activists than we are.
We are all confined here. We all eat the same food. I'm going to support it.
US TOO!
The next day, in the common prisoners' section...
Wake up, birds. Your food has arrived.
You can take it back to the pigsty where you got it. We're not going to eat this anymore.

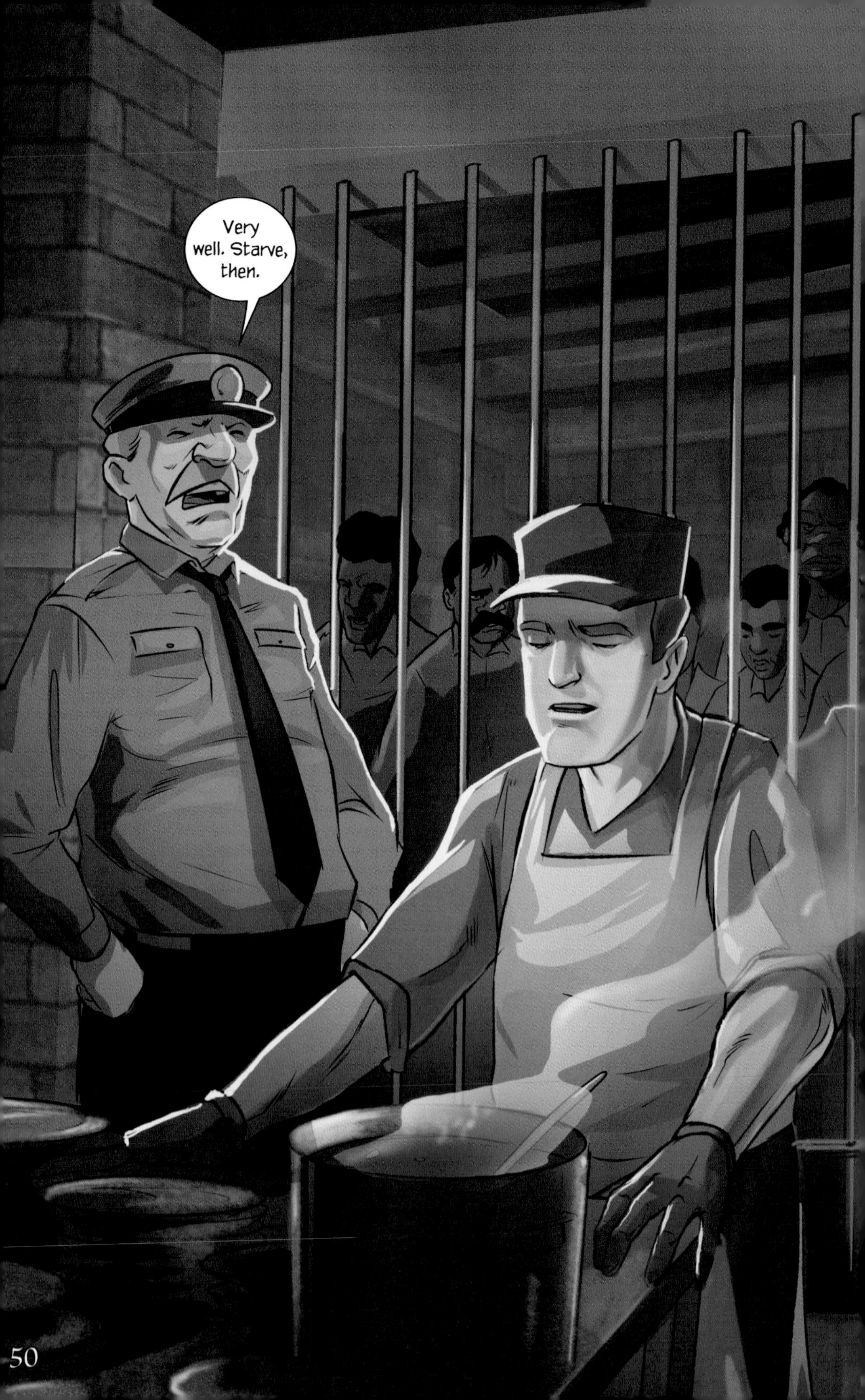
Very well. Starve, then.

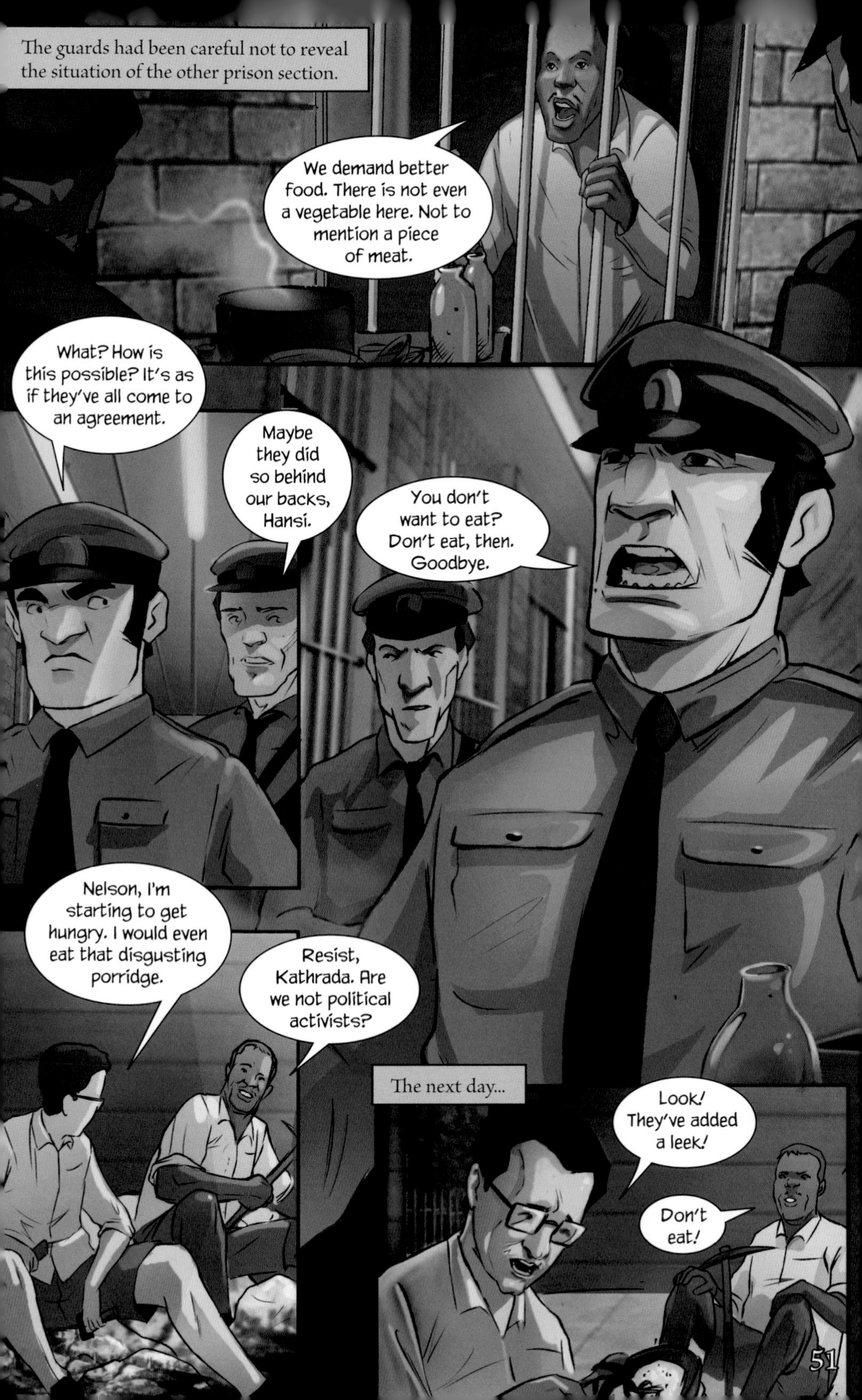
The guards had been careful not to reveal the situation of the other prison section.
We demand better food. There is not even a vegetable here. Not to mention a piece of meat.
What? How is this possible? It's as if they've all come to an agreement.
Maybe they did so behind our backs, Hansi.
You don't want to eat? Don't eat, then. Goodbye.
Nelson, I'm starting to get hungry. I would even eat that disgusting porridge.
Resist, Kathrada. Are we not political activists?
The next day...
Look! They've added a leek!
Don't eat!

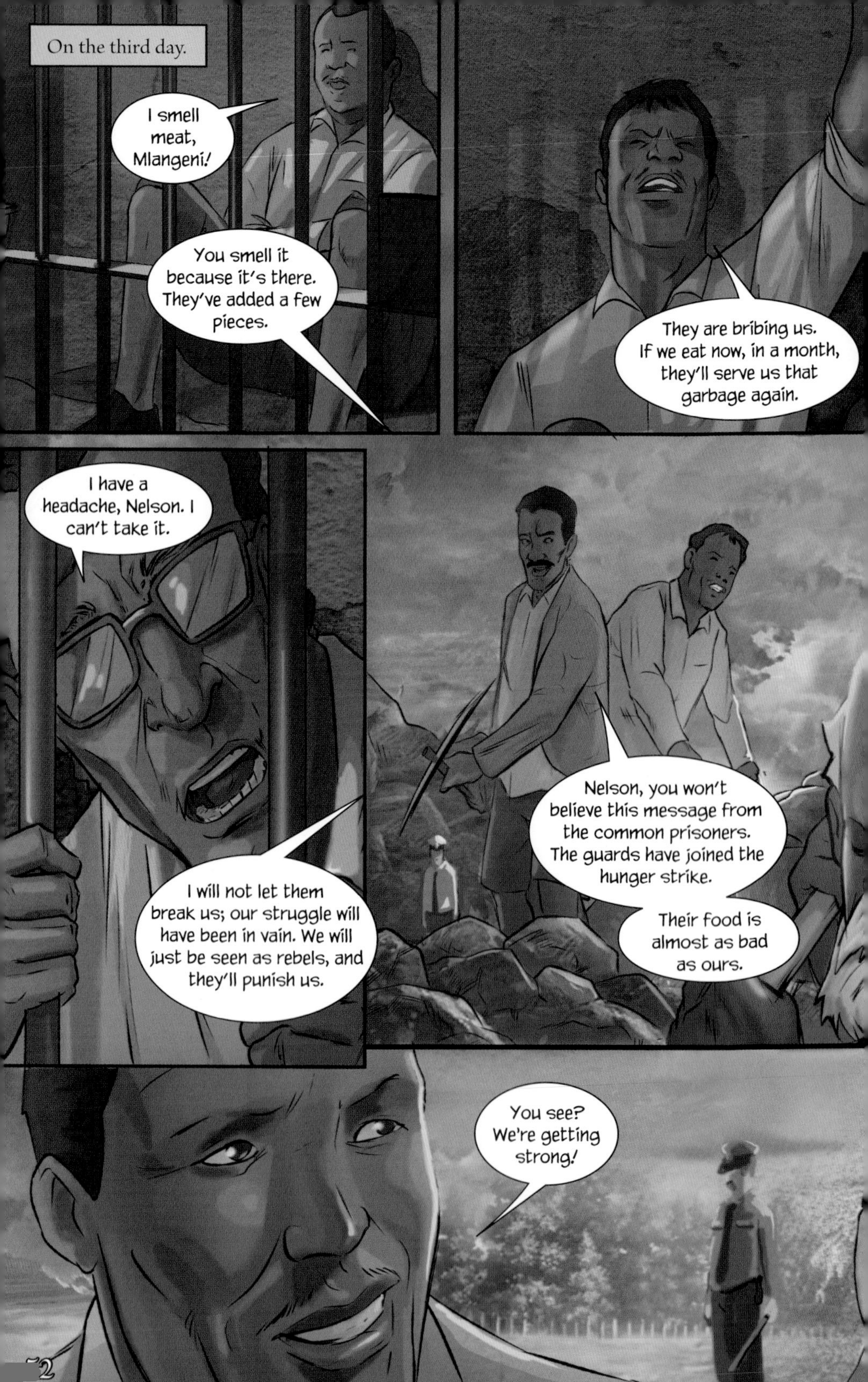
On the third day.
I smell meat, Mlangeni!
You smell it because it's there. They've added a few pieces.
They are bribing us. If we eat now, in a month, they'll serve us that garbage again.
I have a headache, Nelson. I can't take it.
I will not let them break us; our struggle will have been in vain. We will just be seen as rebels, and they'll punish us.
Nelson, you won't believe this message from the common prisoners. The guards have joined the hunger strike.
Their food is almost as bad as ours.
You see? We're getting strong!

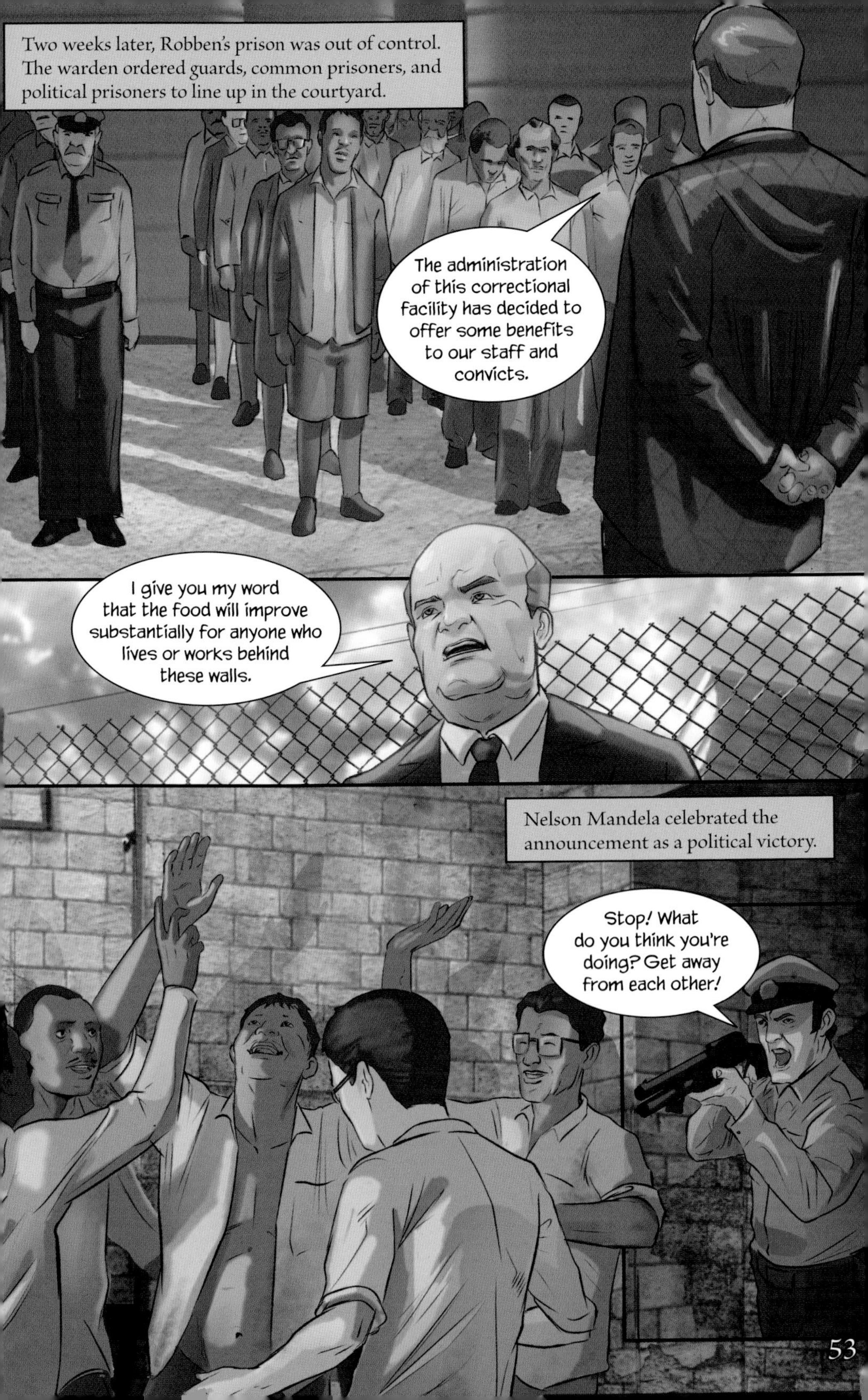

Two weeks later, Robben's prison was out of control. The warden ordered guards, common prisoners, and political prisoners to line up in the courtyard.
The administration of this correctional facility has decided to offer some benefits to our staff and convicts.
I give you my word that the food will improve substantially for anyone who lives or works behind these walls.
Nelson Mandela celebrated the announcement as a political victory.
Stop! What do you think you're doing? Get away from each other!

CHAPTER 6
AFRIKA MAYIBUYE

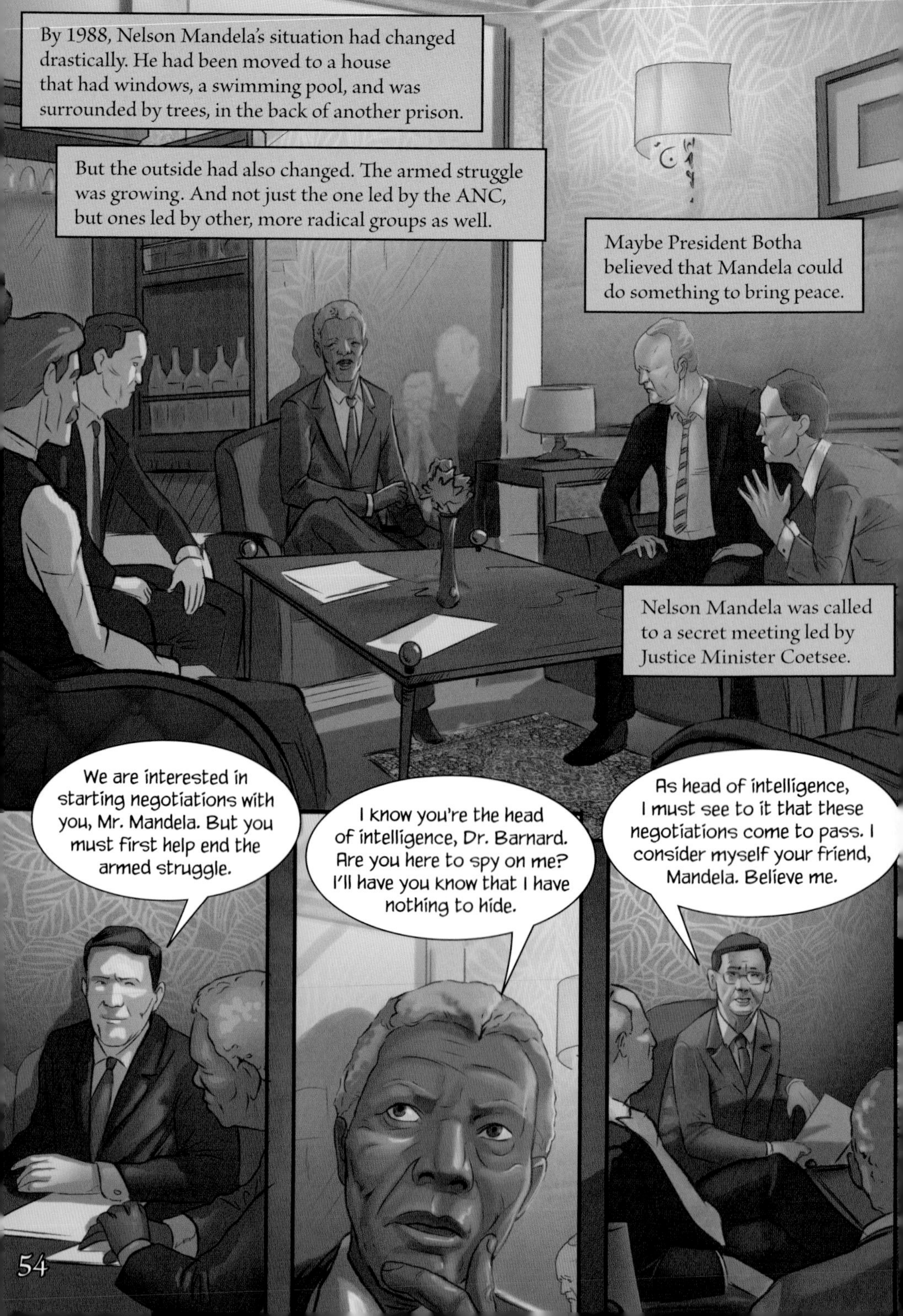
By 1988, Nelson Mandela's situation had changed drastically. He had been moved to a house that had windows, a swimming pool, and was surrounded by trees, in the back of another prison.
But the outside had also changed. The armed struggle was growing. And not just the one led by the ANC, but ones led by other, more radical groups as well.
Maybe President Botha believed that Mandela could do something to bring peace.
Nelson Mandela was called to a secret meeting led by Justice Minister Coetsee.
We are interested in starting negotiations with you, Mr. Mandela. But you must first help end the armed struggle.
I know you're the head of intelligence, Dr. Barnard. Are you here to spy on me? I'll have you know that I have nothing to hide.
As head of intelligence, I must see to it that these negotiations come to pass. I consider myself your friend, Mandela. Believe me.

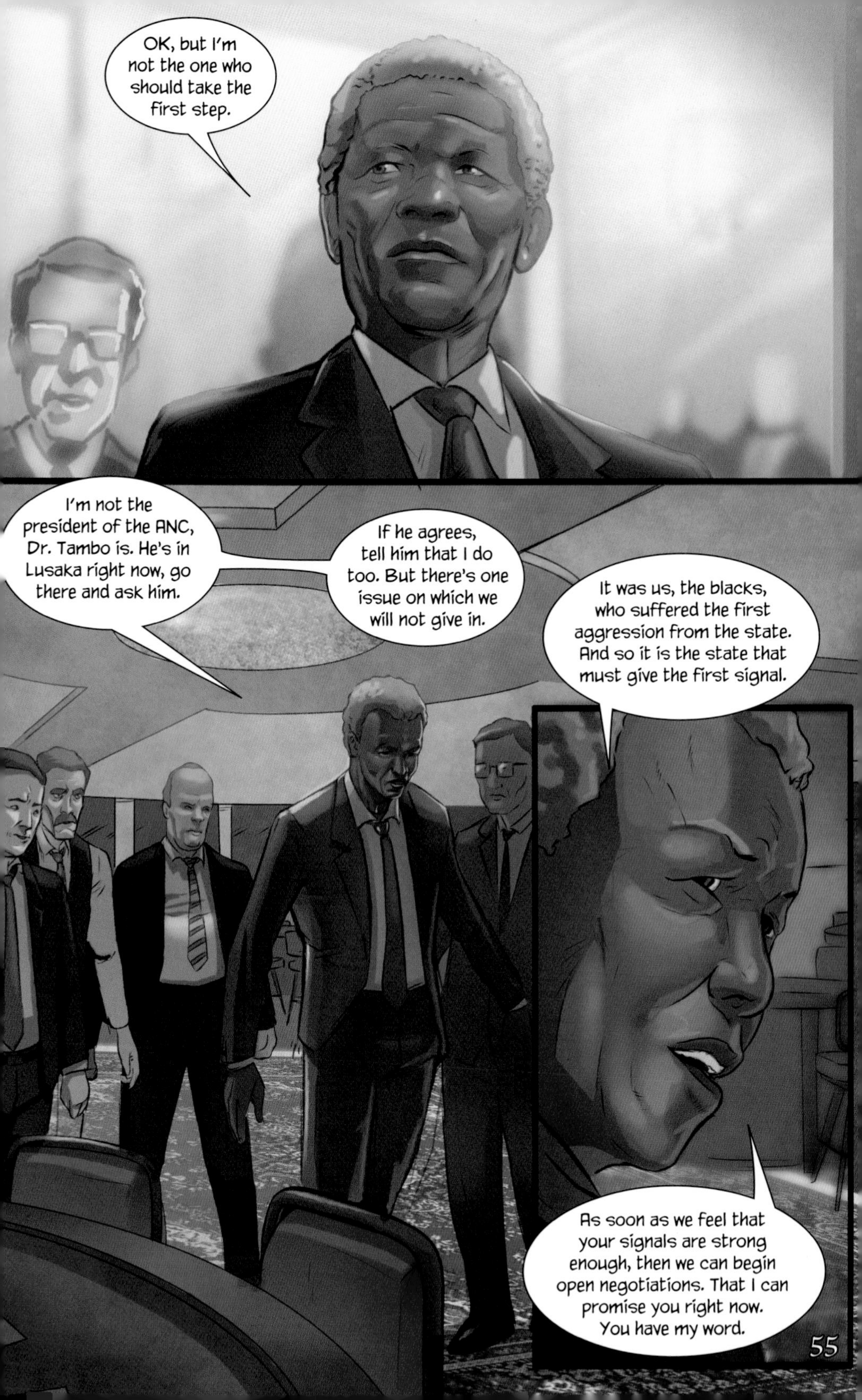
OK, but I'm not the one who should take the first step.
I'm not the president of the ANC, Dr. Tambo is. He's in Lusaka right now, go there and ask him.
If he agrees, tell him that I do too. But there's one issue on which we will not give in.
It was us, the blacks, who suffered the first aggression from the state. And so it is the state that must give the first signal.
As soon as we feel that your signals are strong enough, then we can begin open negotiations. That I can promise you right now. You have my word.

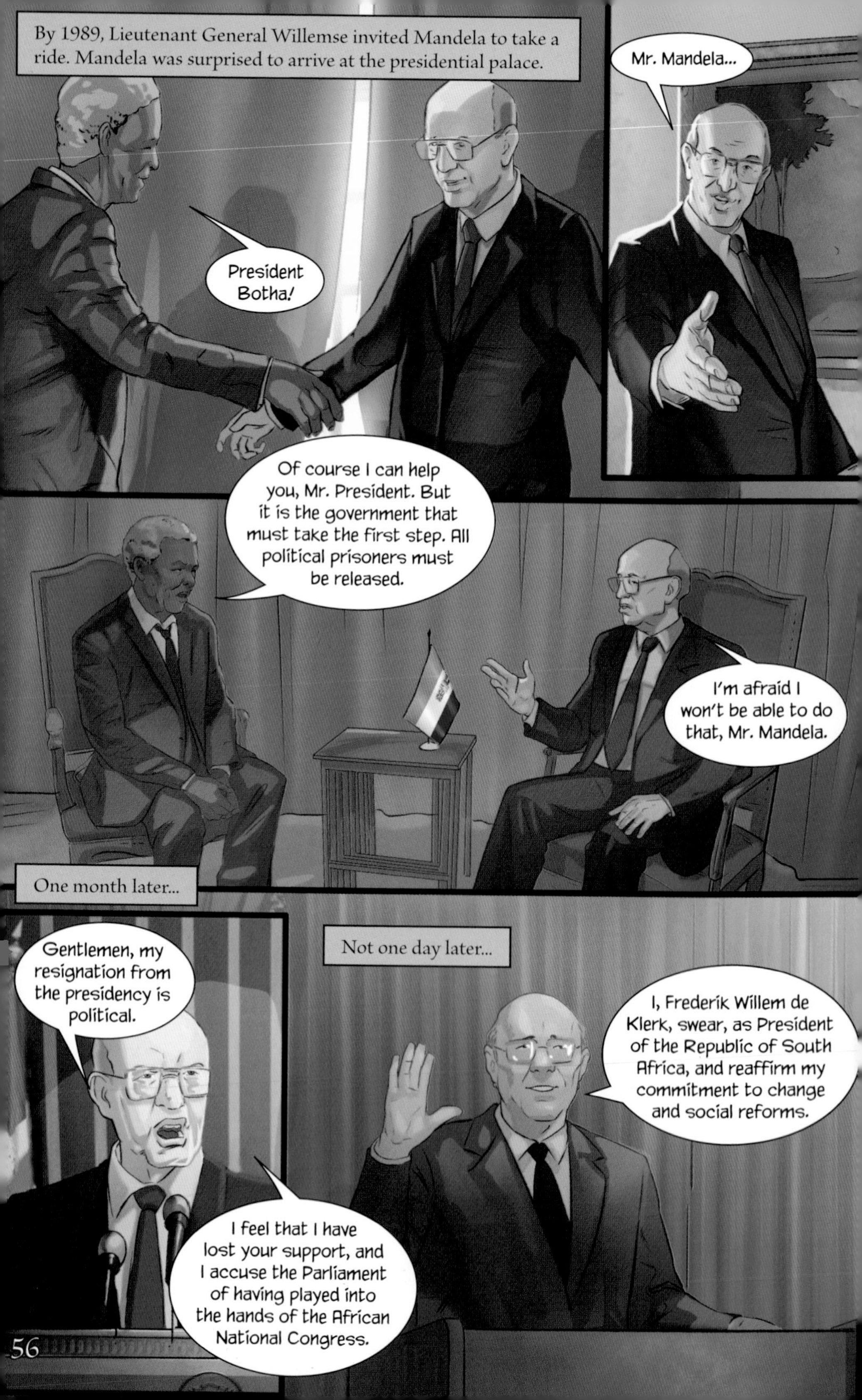
By 1989, Lieutenant General Willemse invited Mandela to take a ride. Mandela was surprised to arrive at the presidential palace.
President Botha!
Mr. Mandela...
Of course I can help you, Mr. President. But it is the government that must take the first step. All political prisoners must be released.
I'm afraid I won't be able to do that, Mr. Mandela.
One month later...
Gentlemen, my resignation from the presidency is political.
I feel that I have lost your support, and I accuse the Parliament of having played into the hands of the African National Congress.
Not one day later...
I, Frederik Willem de Klerk, swear, as President of the Republic of South Africa, and reaffirm my commitment to change and social reforms.

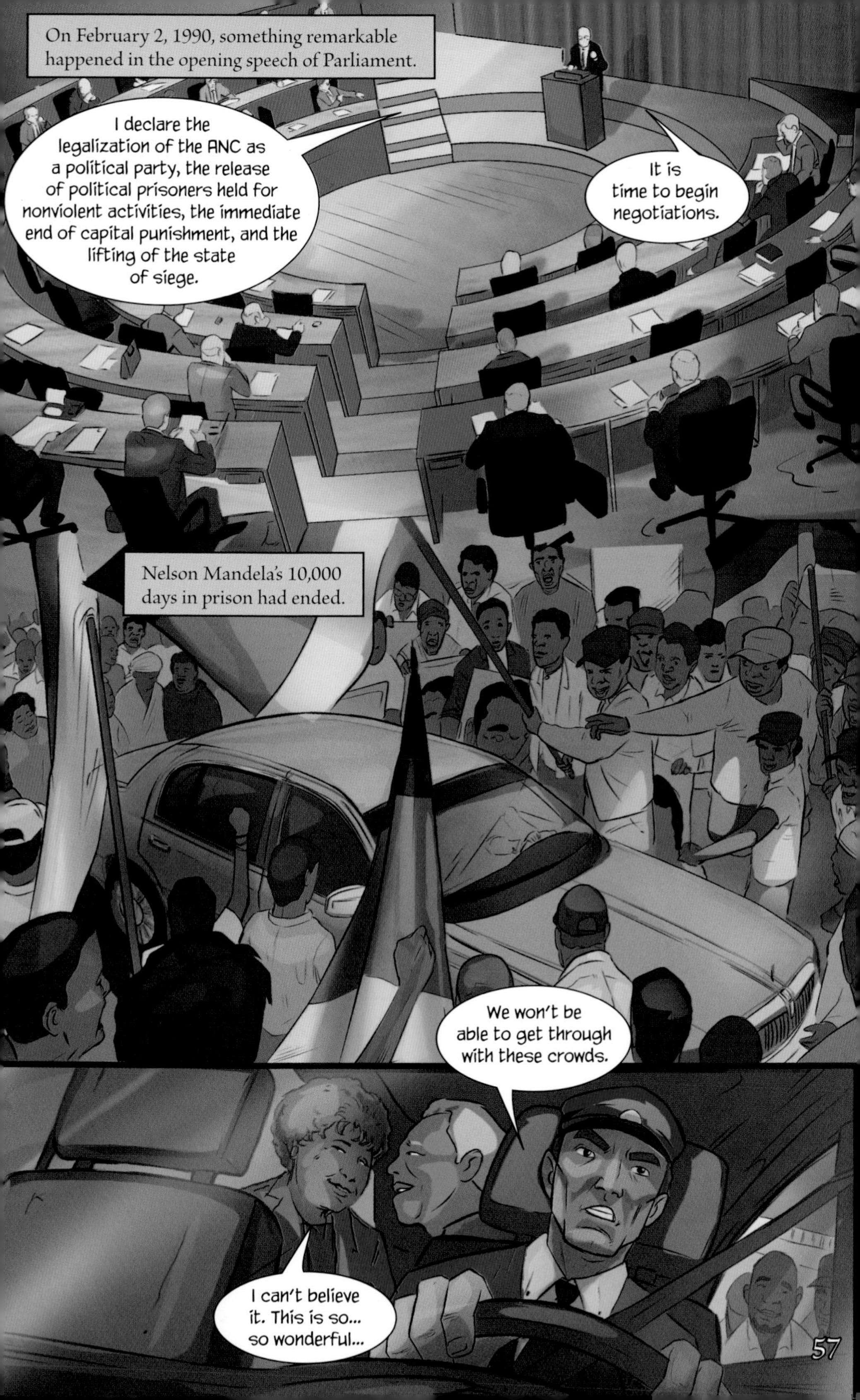
On February 2, 1990, something remarkable happened in the opening speech of Parliament.
I declare the legalization of the ANC as a political party, the release of political prisoners held for nonviolent activities, the immediate end of capital punishment, and the lifting of the state of siege.
It is time to begin negotiations.
Nelson Mandela's 10,000 days in prison had ended.
We won't be able to get through with these crowds.
I can't believe it. This is so... so wonderful...

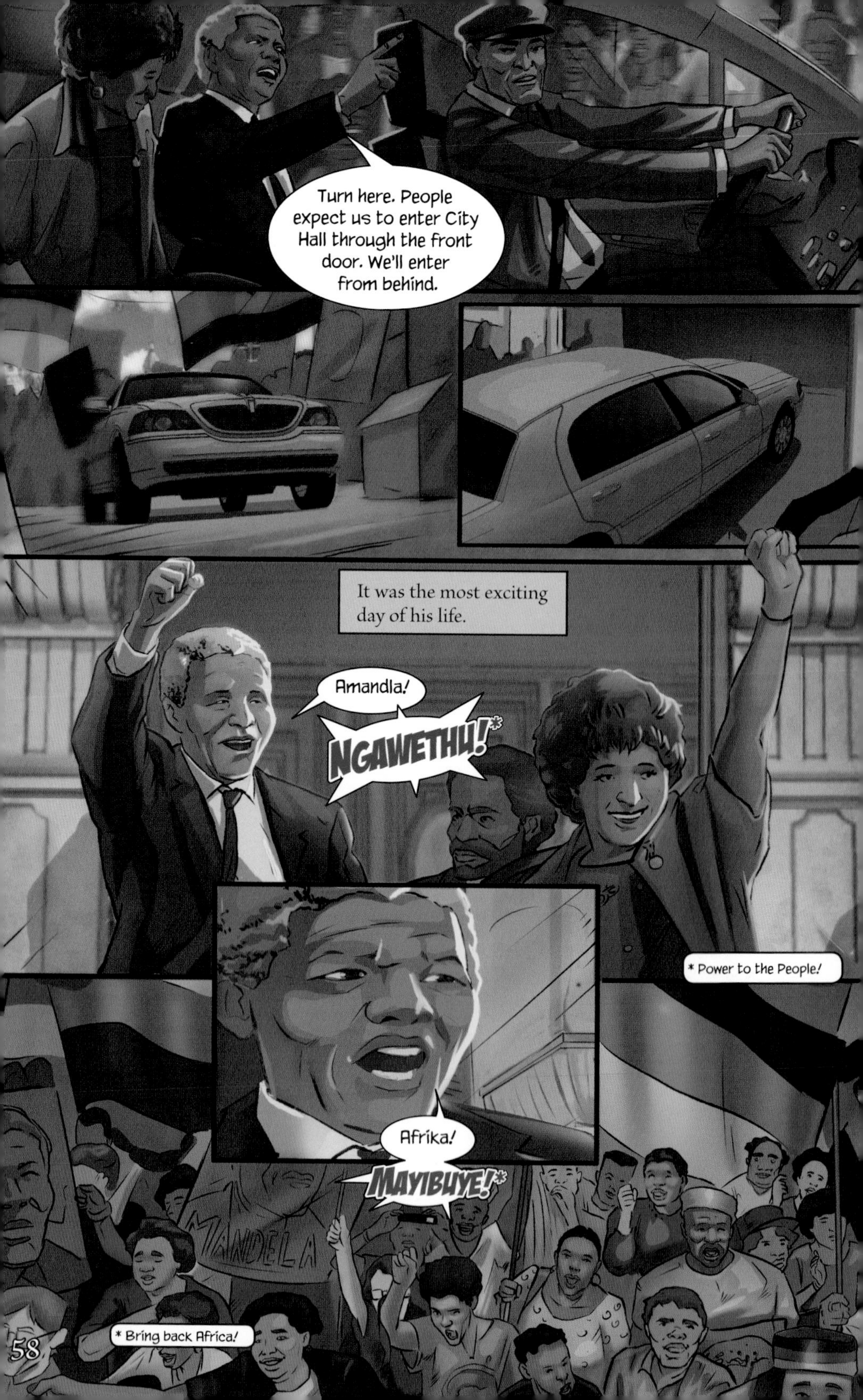
Turn here. People expect us to enter City Hall through the front door. We'll enter from behind.
It was the most exciting day of his life.
Amandla!
NGAWETHU!*
* Power to the People!
Afrika!
MAYIBUYE!*
MANDELA
* Bring back Africa!

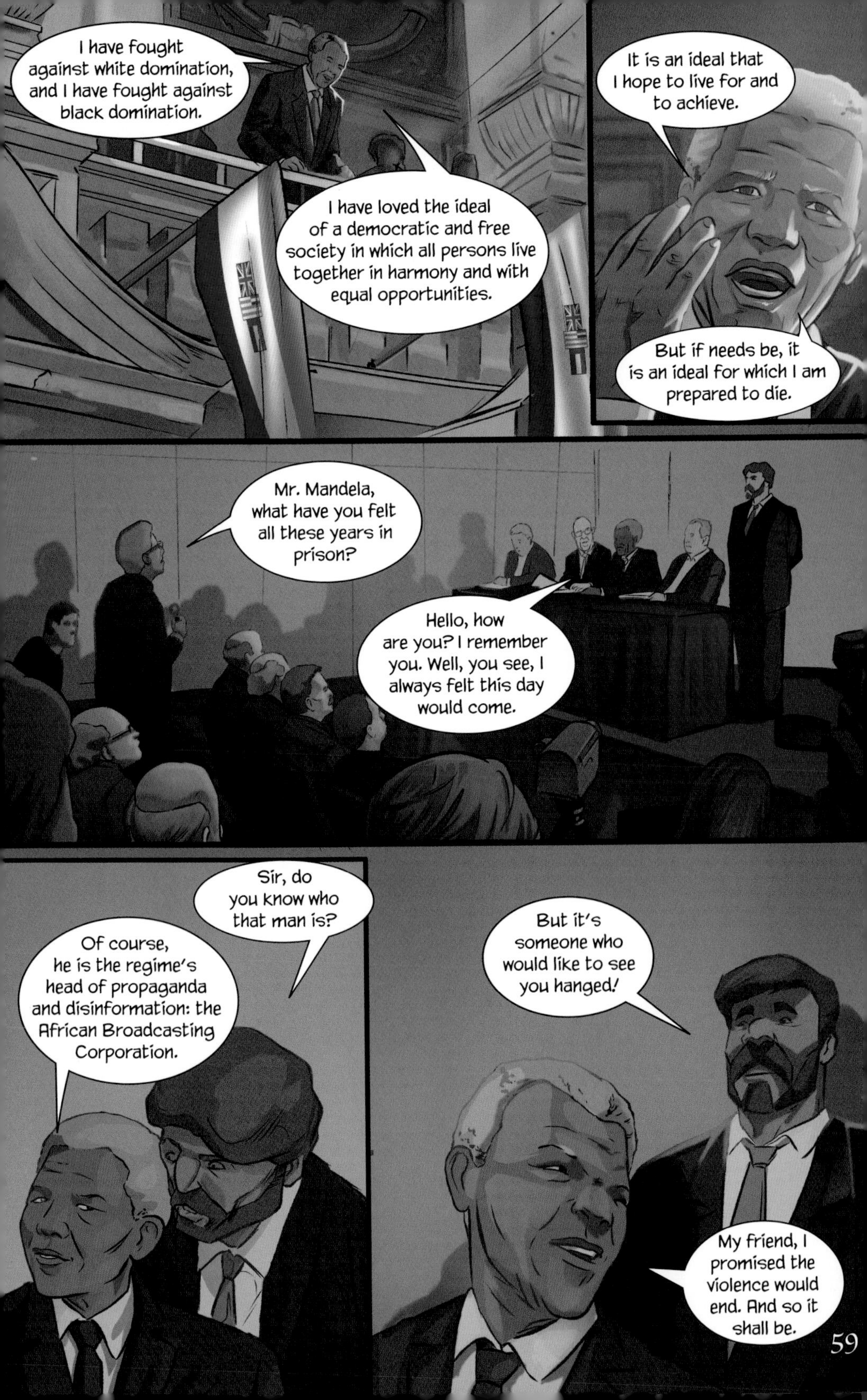
I have fought against white domination, and I have fought against black domination.
I have loved the ideal of a democratic and free society in which all persons live together in harmony and with equal opportunities.
It is an ideal that I hope to live for and to achieve.
But if needs be, it is an ideal for which I am prepared to die.
Mr. Mandela, what have you felt all these years in prison?
Hello, how are you? I remember you. Well, you see, I always felt this day would come.
Sir, do you know who that man is?
Of course, he is the regime's head of propaganda and disinformation: the African Broadcasting Corporation.
But it's someone who would like to see you hanged!
My friend, I promised the violence would end. And so it shall be.

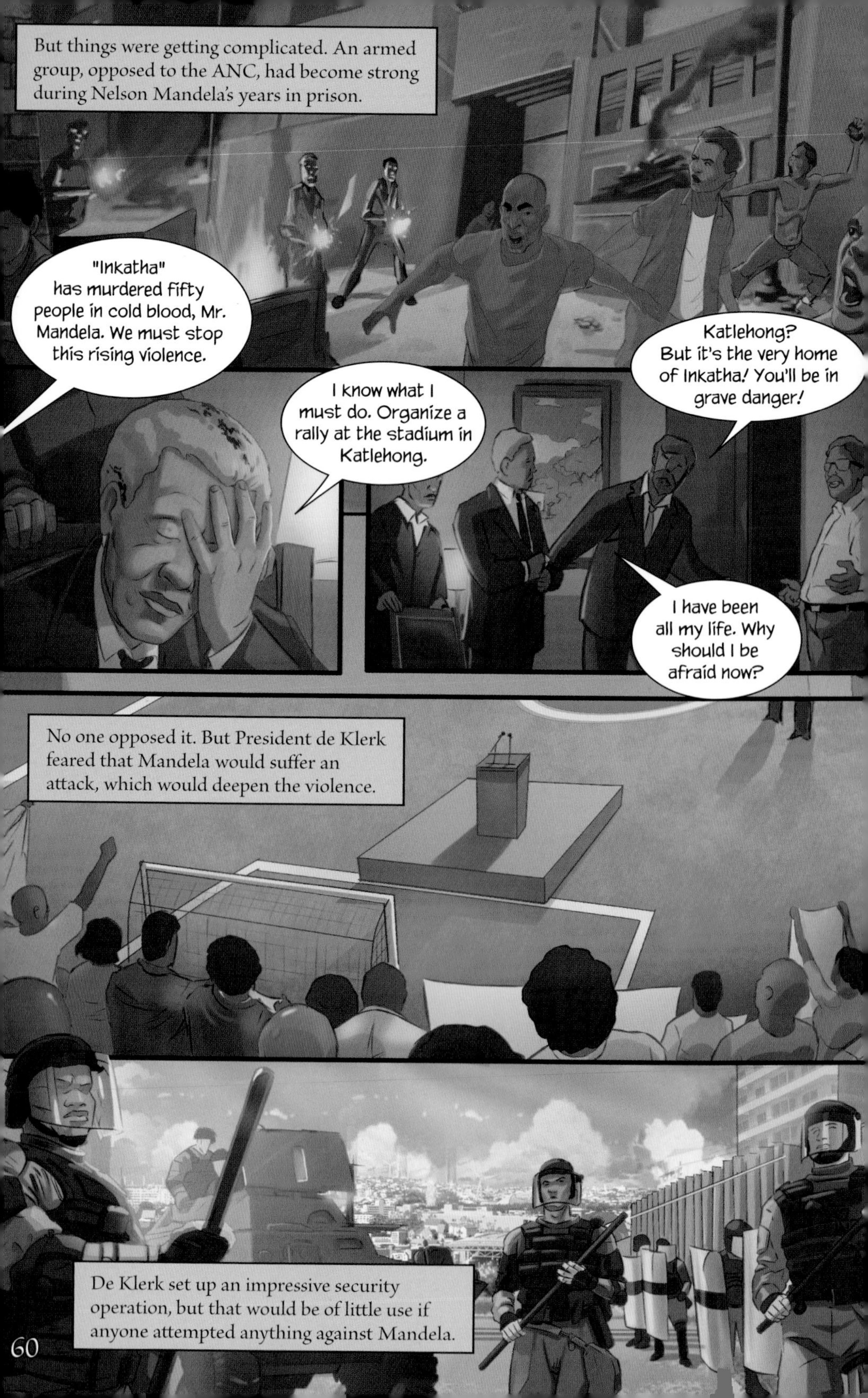
But things were getting complicated. An armed group, opposed to the ANC, had become strong during Nelson Mandela's years in prison.
"Inkatha" has murdered fifty people in cold blood, Mr. Mandela. We must stop this rising violence.
I know what I must do. Organize a rally at the stadium in Katlehong.
Katlehong? But it's the very home of Inkatha! You'll be in grave danger!
I have been all my life. Why should I be afraid now?
No one opposed it. But President de Klerk feared that Mandela would suffer an attack, which would deepen the violence.
De Klerk set up an impressive security operation, but that would be of little use if anyone attempted anything against Mandela.

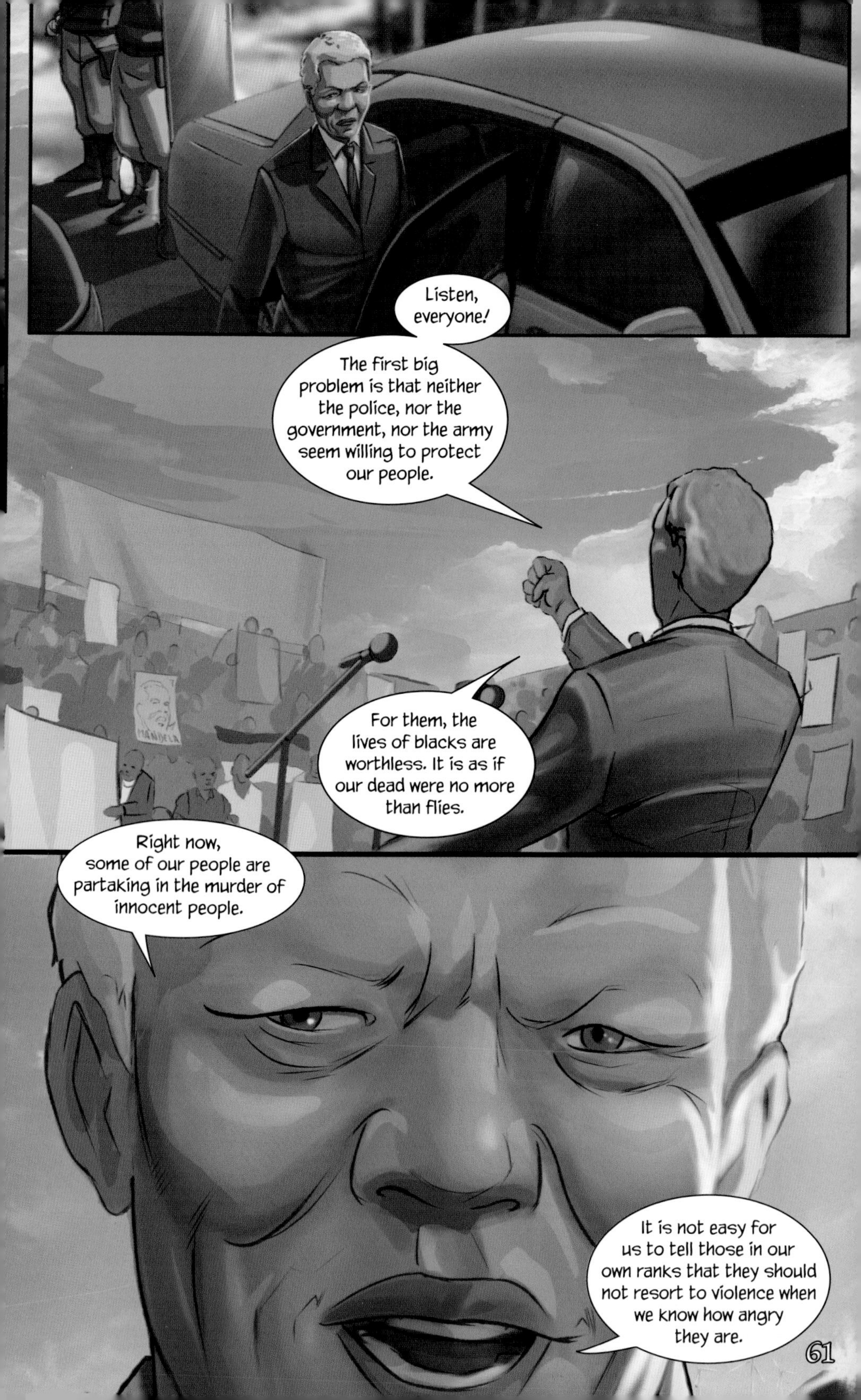
Listen, everyone!
The first big problem is that neither the police, nor the government, nor the army seem willing to protect our people.
MANDELA
For them, the lives of blacks are worthless. It is as if our dead were no more than flies.
Right now, some of our people are partaking in the murder of innocent people.
It is not easy for us to tell those in our own ranks that they should not resort to violence when we know how angry they are.

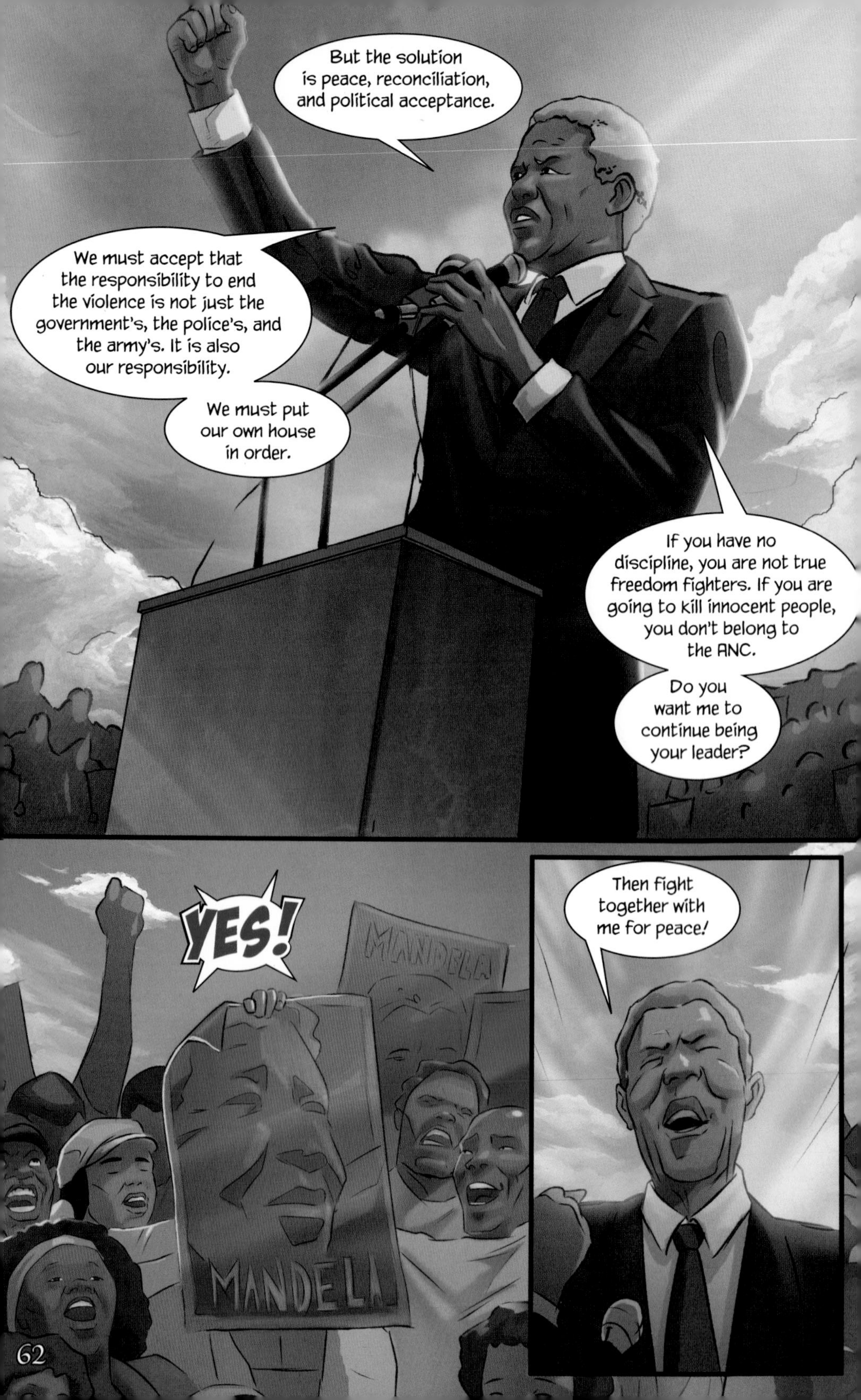
But the solution is peace, reconciliation, and political acceptance.
We must accept that the responsibility to end the violence is not just the government's, the police's, and the army's. It is also our responsibility.
We must put our own house in order.
If you have no discipline, you are not true freedom fighters. If you are going to kill innocent people, you don't belong to the ANC.
Do you want me to continue being your leader?
YES!
MANDELA
MANDELA
Then fight together with me for peace!

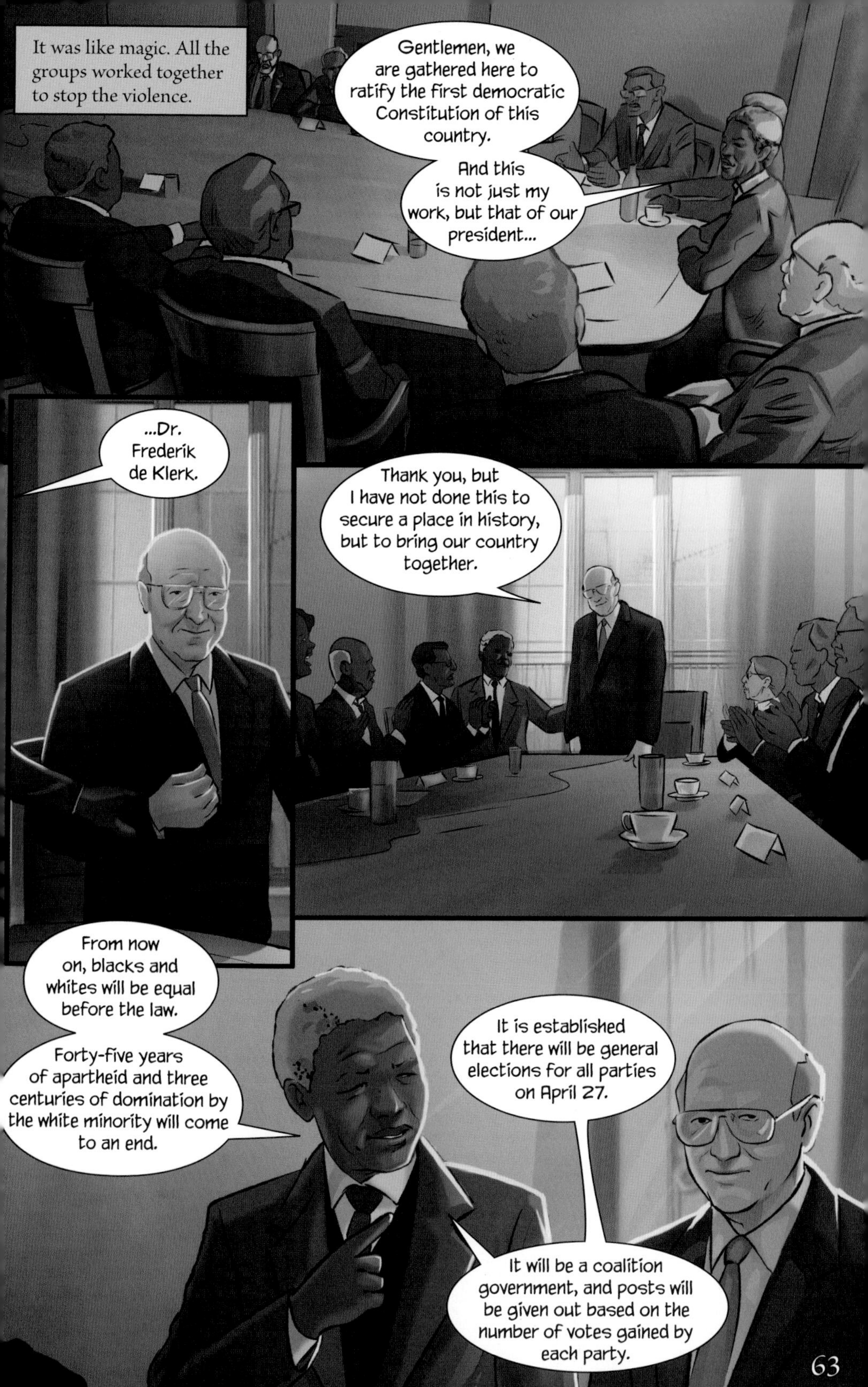
It was like magic. All the groups worked together to stop the violence.
Gentlemen, we are gathered here to ratify the first democratic Constitution of this country.
And this is not just my work, but that of our president...
...Dr. Frederik de Klerk.
Thank you, but I have not done this to secure a place in history, but to bring our country together.
From now on, blacks and whites will be equal before the law.
Forty-five years of apartheid and three centuries of domination by the white minority will come to an end.
It is established that there will be general elections for all parties on April 27.
It will be a coalition government, and posts will be given out based on the number of votes gained by each party.

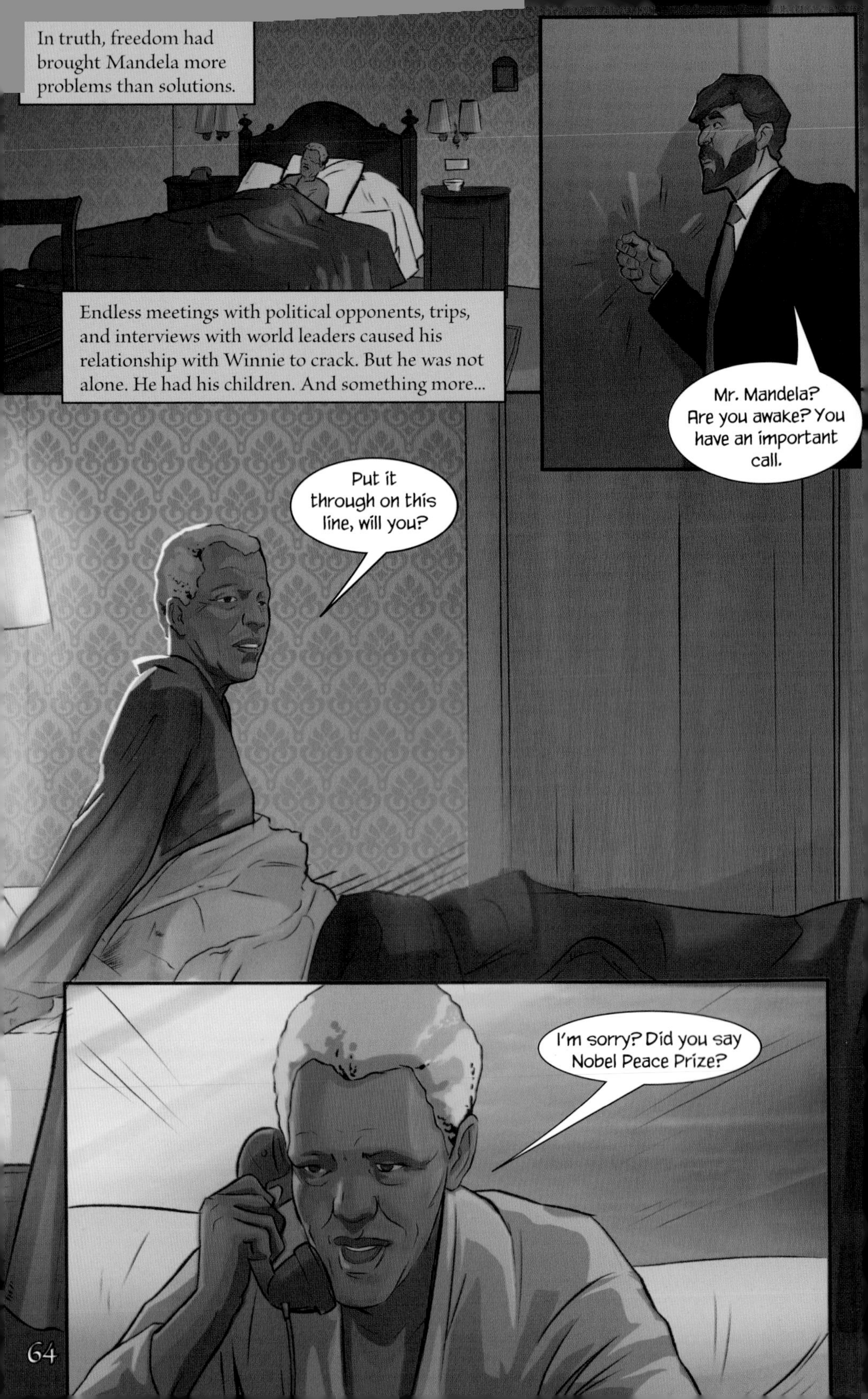
In truth, freedom had brought Mandela more problems than solutions.
Endless meetings with political opponents, trips, and interviews with world leaders caused his relationship with Winnie to crack. But he was not alone. He had his children. And something more...
Mr. Mandela? Are you awake? You have an important call.
Put it through on this line, will you?
I'm sorry? Did you say Nobel Peace Prize?

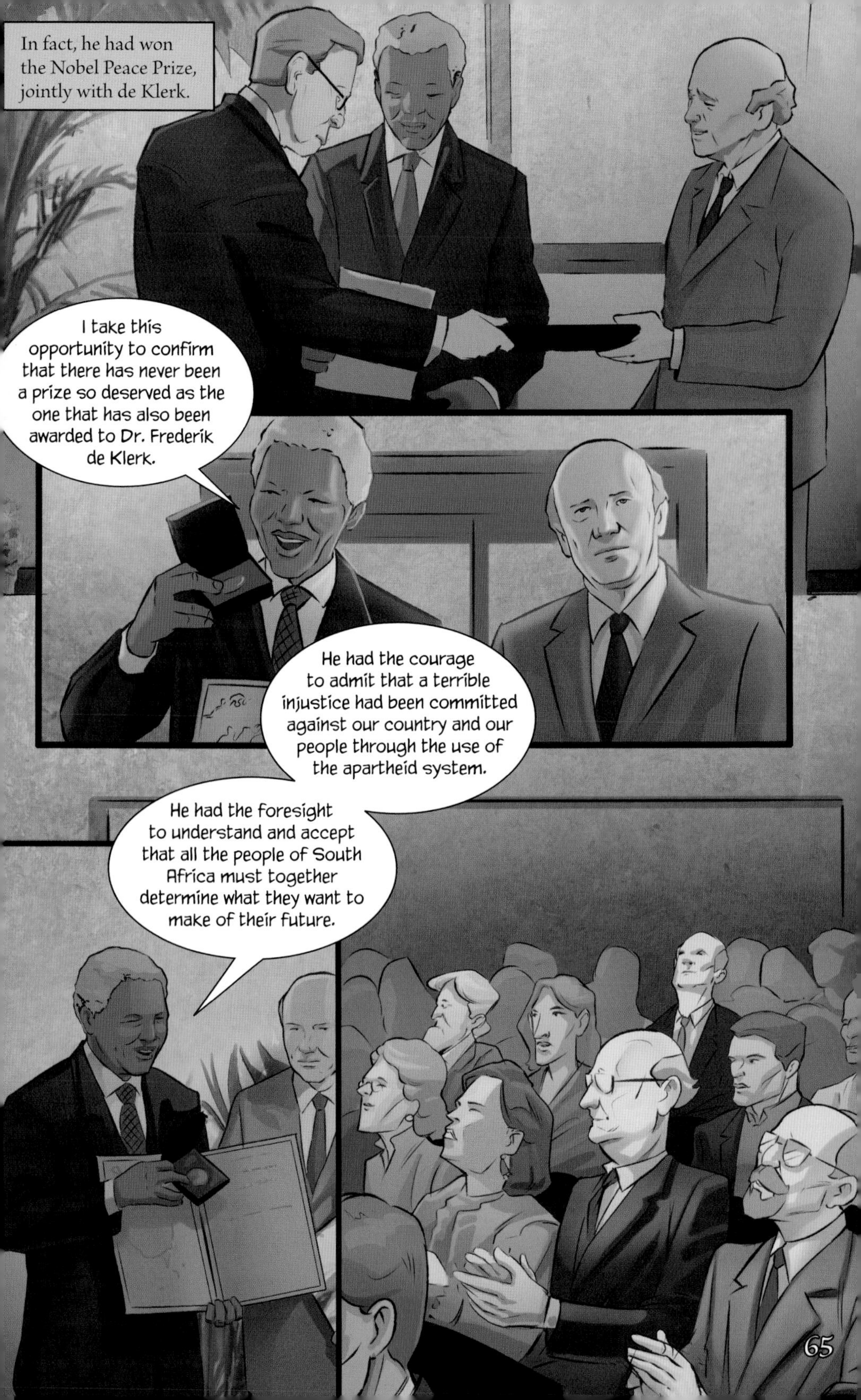
In fact, he had won the Nobel Peace Prize, jointly with de Klerk.
I take this opportunity to confirm that there has never been a prize so deserved as the one that has also been awarded to Dr. Frederik de Klerk.
He had the courage to admit that a terrible injustice had been committed against our country and our people through the use of the apartheid system.
He had the foresight to understand and accept that all the people of South Africa must together determine what they want to make of their future.

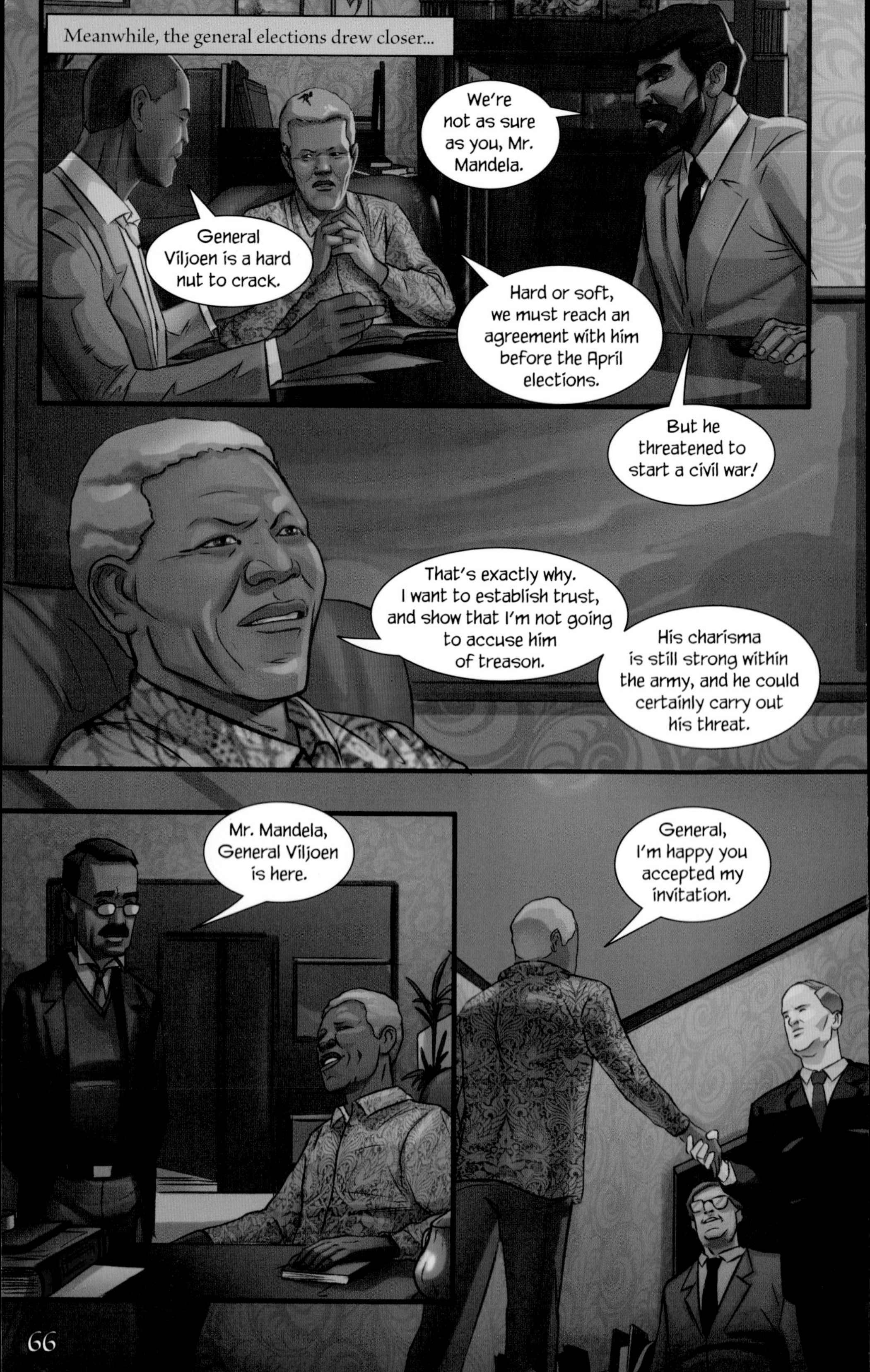
Meanwhile, the general elections drew closer...
We're not as sure as you, Mr. Mandela.
General Viljoen is a hard nut to crack.
Hard or soft, we must reach an agreement with him before the April elections.
But he threatened to start a civil war!
That's exactly why. I want to establish trust, and show that I'm not going to accuse him of treason.
His charisma is still strong within the army, and he could certainly carry out his threat.
Mr. Mandela, General Viljoen is here.
General, I'm happy you accepted my invitation.

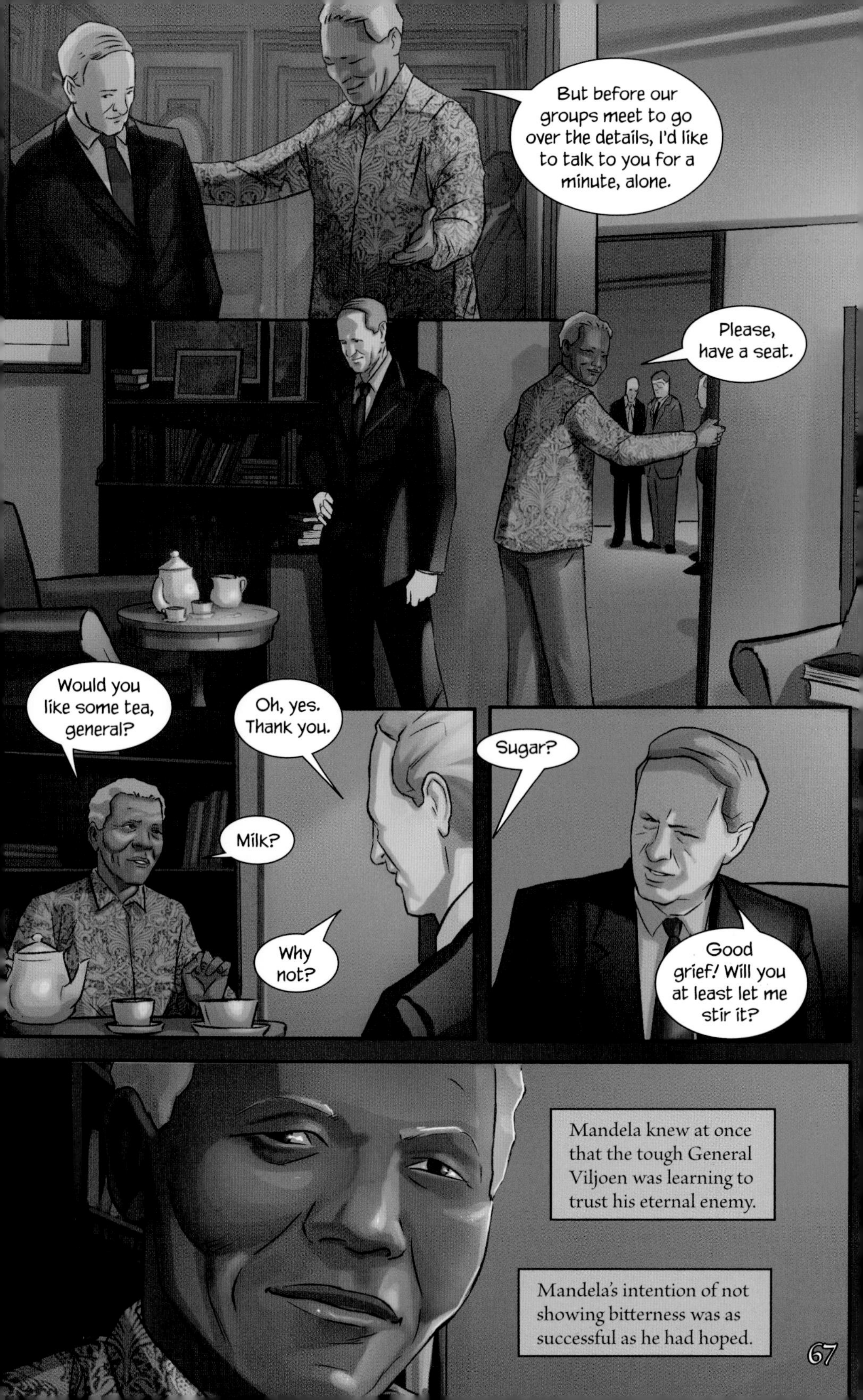
But before our groups meet to go over the details, I'd like to talk to you for a minute, alone.
Please, have a seat.
Would you like some tea, general?
Oh, yes. Thank you.
Milk?
Why not?
Sugar?
Good grief! Will you at least let me stir it?
Mandela knew at once that the tough General Viljoen was learning to trust his eternal enemy.
Mandela's intention of not showing bitterness was as successful as he had hoped.

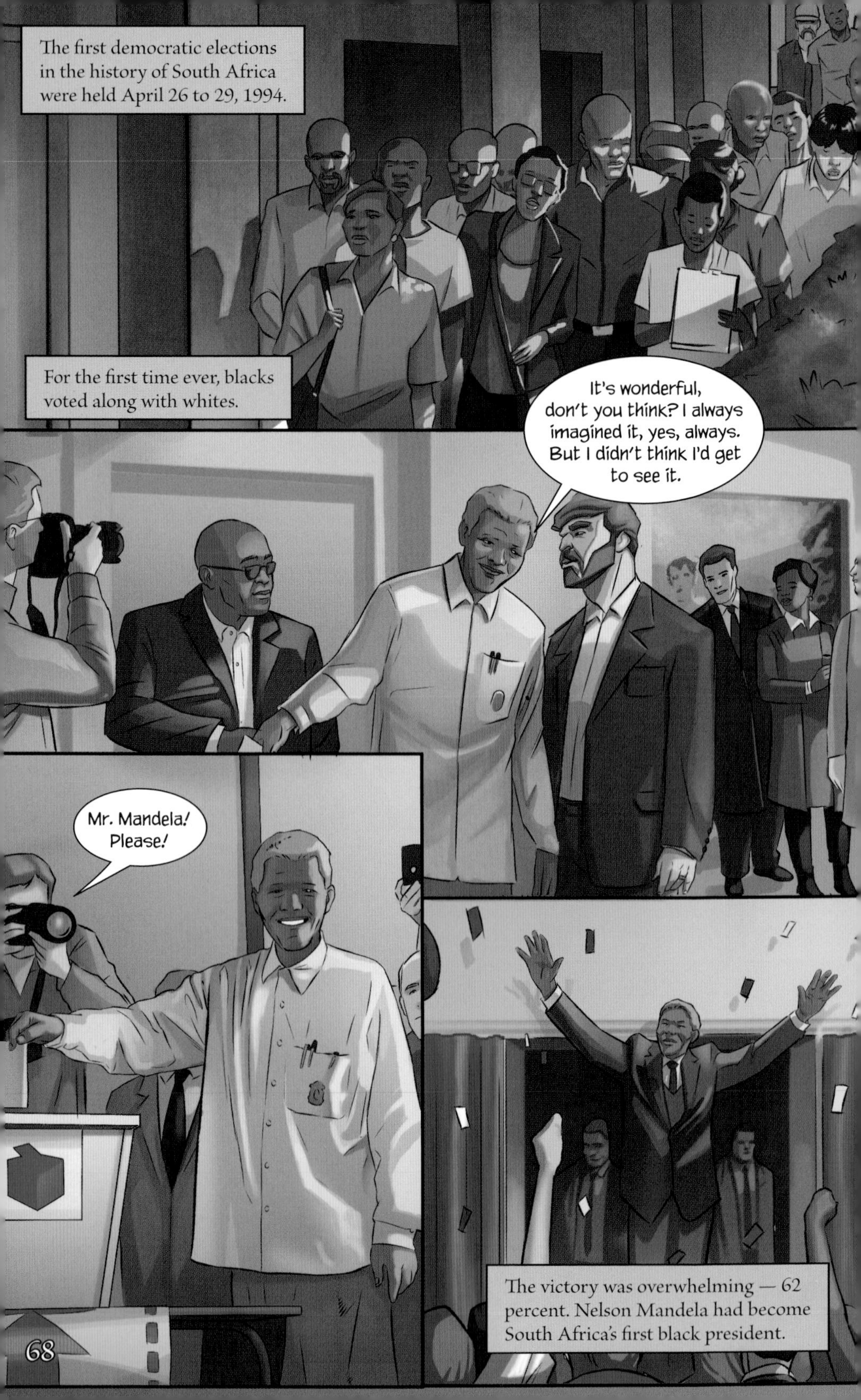
The first democratic elections in the history of South Africa were held April 26 to 29, 1994.
For the first time ever, blacks voted along with whites.
It's wonderful, don't you think? I always imagined it, yes, always. But I didn't think I'd get to see it.
Mr. Mandela! Please!
The victory was overwhelming — 62 percent. Nelson Mandela had become South Africa's first black president.

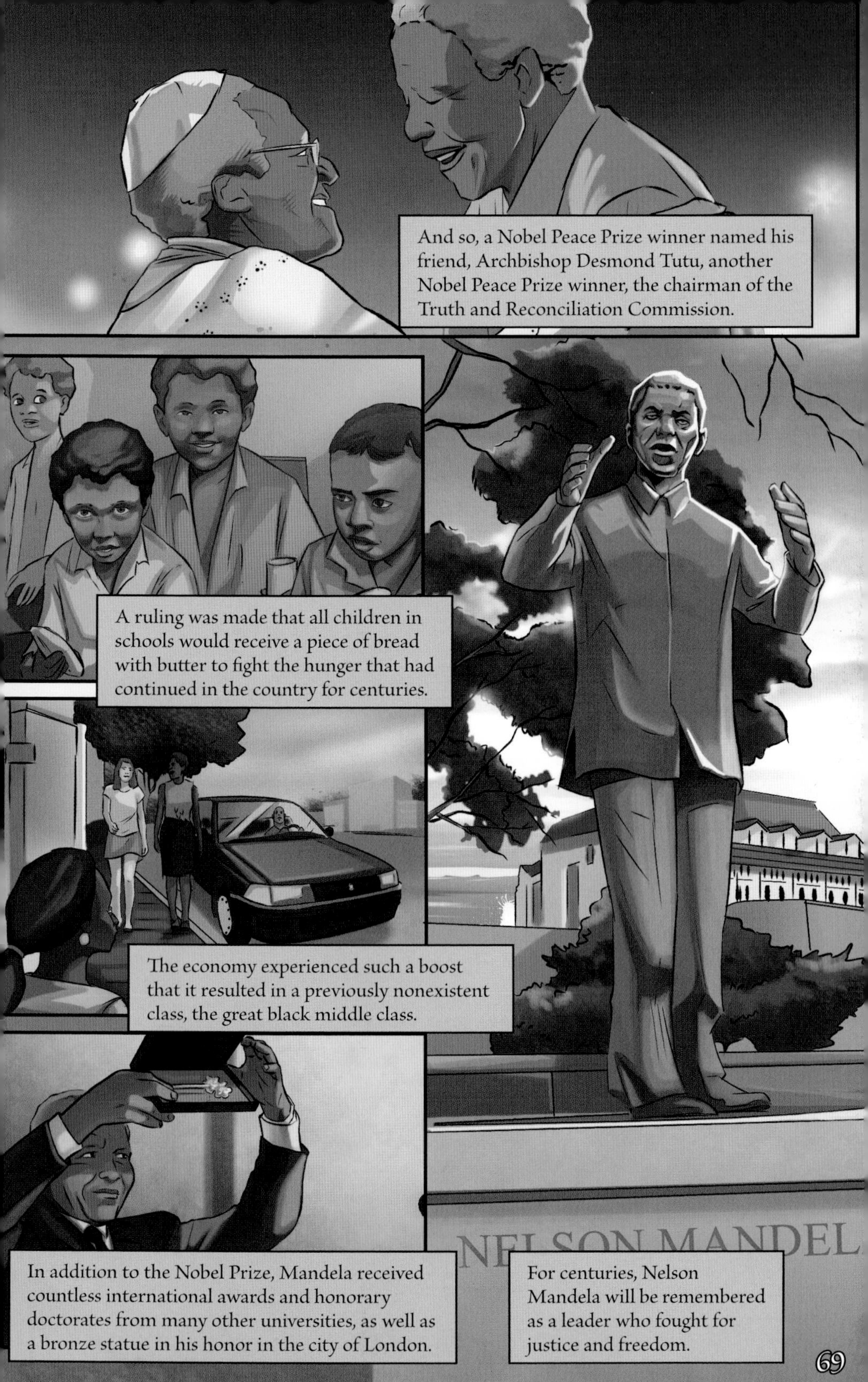
And so, a Nobel Peace Prize winner named his friend, Archbishop Desmond Tutu, another Nobel Peace Prize winner, the chairman of the Truth and Reconciliation Commission.
A ruling was made that all children in schools would receive a piece of bread with butter to fight the hunger that had continued in the country for centuries.
The economy experienced such a boost that it resulted in a previously nonexistent class, the great black middle class.
In addition to the Nobel Prize, Mandela received countless international awards and honorary doctorates from many other universities, as well as a bronze statue in his honor in the city of London.
NELSON MANDEL
For centuries, Nelson Mandela will be remembered as a leader who fought for justice and freedom.

TIMELINE
1918-2013

1918	1930s	1940s	1950s
Mandela is born on July 18, 1918, in the village of Mvezo, with the name Rolihlahla Mandela. He is the son of the chief adviser to the Thembu king. In 1925, he attends school, where his teacher renames him Nelson.	Mandela's father dies, and he is handed over to the care of the Thembu regent, Jongintaba Dalindyebo. In 1934, he attends the Clarkebury Institute. In 1937, Wesleyan College. In 1939, he enrolls at University College, Fort Hare.	Mandela is expelled for joining a student protest. In 1941, he moves to Johannesburg, escaping an arranged marriage. He meets Walter Sisulu and, in 1942, works at the law firm of Witkin, Sidelsky, and Eidelman. In 1943, he completes his studies at the University of South Africa. In 1944, he co-founds the Youth League of the African National Congress (ANC) and gets married for the first time. He begins his law studies, which he will leave and return to over the years.	First convictions for Mandela's political activity. In 1952, he is sentenced to nine months of forced labor for a civil disobedience campaign against unjust laws. In 1953, he designs a plan for the ANC's future secret actions. He is arrested again in 1955 and found not guilty in 1956, after the trial.

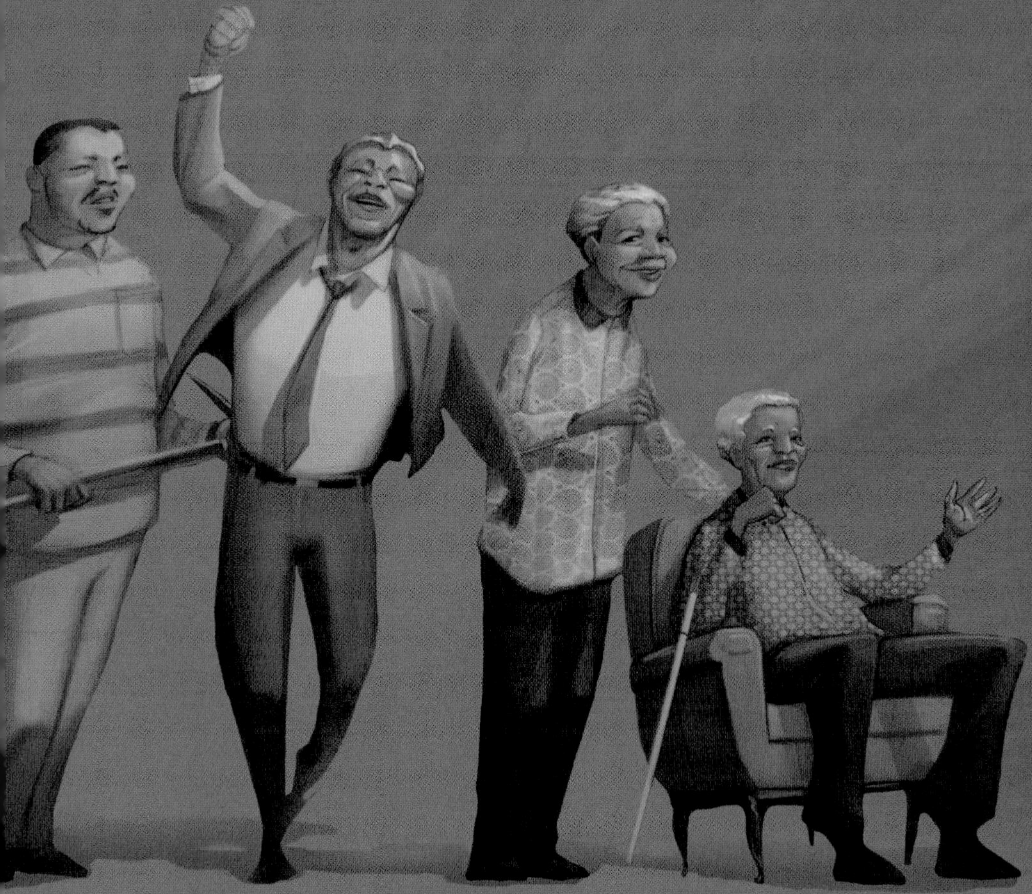

1960s	1980s	1990s	2000
Banning of the ANC, which goes underground. In 1961, Mandela founds the armed wing of the ANC, Umkhonto we Sizwe. In 1962, he travels to Morocco and Ethiopia for military training. He is arrested upon returning to South Africa and is sentenced to five years in prison. In 1963, the Rivonia Trial is held. Mandela is sentenced to life imprisonment in 1964 and sent to Robben Island.	In 1982, Mandela is moved to Pollsmoor Prison. In 1985, he rejects President Botha's first release offer. In 1988, after several health issues and being diagnosed with tuberculosis, he is sent to Victor Verster Prison, where he spends 14 months in a house. In 1989, he earns his law degree from the University of South Africa.	End of the ban on the ANC. Mandela is released from prison and elected president of the ANC. In 1993, he receives the Nobel Peace Prize, shared with President de Klerk. In 1994, he votes for the first time in his life, along with the rest of the black population of South Africa. He is elected president of the Republic of South Africa. In 1999, he ends his term and retires from politics.	In 2003, Mandela starts the Mandela Rhodes Foundation. He retires from public life in 2004. In 2008, he asks future generations to continue fighting for social justice. He dies on December 5, 2013, in Johannesburg.

Souce: www.nelsonmandela.org/content/page/timeline

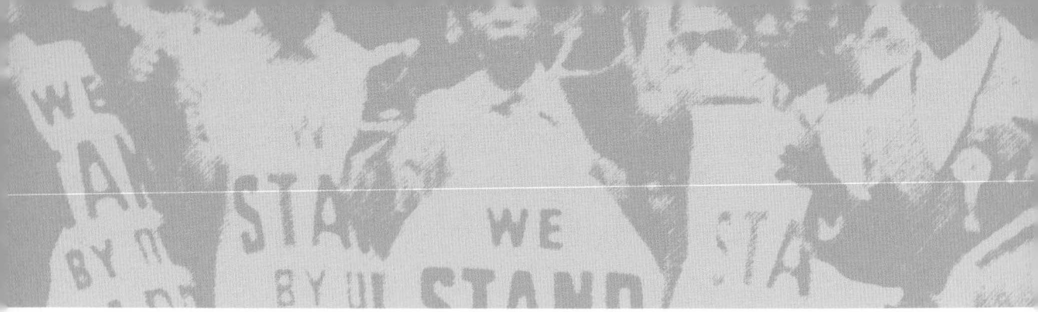
WE

WHO WAS NELSON MANDELA?

Nelson Mandela was one of the most important political figures of the 20th century. He was an example to the world when it comes to searching for peace.

Mandela was born in 1918, and, from an early age, looked to the leaders of his tribe, the Thembu, as his mentors. He began his own political career at age 24 when he joined the African National Congress (ANC). This organization carried out peaceful campaigns against the apartheid system, which subjected South Africa's black population to discrimination and segregation. In 1943, Mandela founded the ANC's Youth League, carrying out civil disobedience campaigns protesting government decisions against blacks. During these years, he was arrested and sentenced to forced labor.

In the 1960s, the ANC's political activity was banned. Nelson Mandela went on to form an armed wing of the party to resist government repression. As part of his military training, he secretly traveled to Ethiopia, the only African country that had never been subjected to European colonialism. Upon returning, he was arrested and sentenced to life in prison during the famous Rivonia Trial. He was sent to Robben Island, where he stayed for more than 20 years.

In 1990, Mandela was released after the ban on the ANC was lifted. In 1993, he was awarded the Nobel Peace Prize, and, in 1994, he was elected the first black president of the Republic of South Africa.

During his presidency, Mandela forgave those who had abused his people for so many years. He did so for the sake of the peaceful rebuilding of his nation. His words during the Rivonia Trial in 1964 were a perfect example of his life's purpose: "I have fought against white domination, and I have fought against black domination. I have cherished the ideal of a democratic and free society in which all persons live together in harmony and with equal opportunities. It is an ideal to live for and to achieve. But if needs be, it is an ideal for which I am prepared to die."

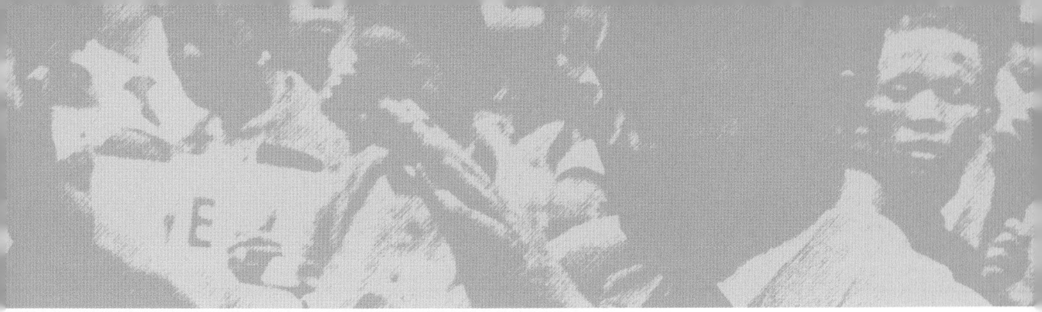

MANDELA AND THE MOVIES

Nelson Mandela has often been depicted in films, TV series, and TV movies throughout the years. His life was, without a doubt, worth remembering on film. One of the first movies to portray his life was a TV film, made in 1987, when Mandela was still in jail. Danny Glover played Mandela in that version.

The year 1997 saw the release of the movie *Mandela and de Klerk,* which looks at Mandela's life from his time in Robben Island until his release. Mandela was played by American actor Sidney Poitier, who, in 1963, was the first African American to win an Oscar for best actor. De Klerk was played by Michael Caine, who, in 1975, had already starred opposite Poitier in a film about apartheid, *The Wilby Conspiracy.*

The most recent biopic about Mandela is *Mandela: Long Walk to Freedom.* The movie is based on Nelson Mandela's autobiography, which shares the same title. Mandela's character was played by British actor Idris Elba, but the first choice was Morgan Freeman.

Coincidentally, Morgan Freeman played Mandela in *Invictus,* a thrilling film directed by Clint Eastwood, which is about President Mandela's support of the South African rugby team during the 1994 World Cup. In this sport, which was practiced only by whites, Mandela saw a chance to unite the entire South African people and heal the wounds of so many years of discrimination and violence.

Nelson Mandela was not only a character in movies, but he also participated as an actor in the film *Malcolm X.* In it he makes a brief appearance as a schoolteacher in South Africa.

SOUTH AFRICA AND APARTHEID

In Afrikaans, the Dutch variant language used in South Africa, "apartheid" means "separation." It was a system of racial discrimination in South Africa from 1948 until 1990.

At that time, only 21 percent of the South African population was white. But it had imposed its control over the black and mixed-race majority since the previous century.

In 1948, after Daniel François Malan was elected prime minister, a mandatory racial registry was established to separate the population. Marriages between blacks and whites were officially banned in 1949. The main goal of the ban was to separate the races by giving whites more legal power than anyone else, but the separation also applied to where people lived. By 1950, only whites could live in certain urban areas, which forced large numbers of blacks to move to rural areas.

At the same time, cities had "whites-only" and "blacks-only" sections, the latter being of lower quality. Segregation reached its highest levels when, in 1959, blacks were assigned to small segregated territories called the Bantustans. They were also denied South African citizenship.

In addition, as of 1954, the black population was fully banned from taking part in political life. This included a ban on holding positions at any level of government, as well as a ban on voting, except for some exclusively black institutions.

Public transportation was also segregated. In the 1950s, Nelson Mandela organized a civil disobedience campaign within the African National Congress against all these limitations, actions that led to his first arrests.

Until the 1960s, protests took the form of passive resistance of the government. People organized marches protesting segregation, and these were generally met with violence by the government. This changed with the banning of the black majority parties, the African National Congress and the African Congress Party. From then on, passive resistance turned into armed struggle. Nelson Mandela became the leader and organizer of his party's armed wing. But in 1963, with a state of national emergency having been declared, he and many other political leaders were arrested and sentenced to life in prison.

During the 1970s, violence peaked during the events known as the "Soweto Massacre." In 1974, the government ruled that the Afrikaans language was mandatory in all schools, including those of the black population. Two years later, the schools of Soweto, an exclusively black district, rebelled by conducting marches and demonstrations. On June 16, 1976, one of those marches ended in a brutal police action, which left 566 children dead and began a wave of violence throughout South Africa.

At the international level, the South African government became increasingly isolated. The country received strong economic sanctions, or trade limitations, from other nations and was not allowed to take part in the 1964 Olympic Games.

The isolation had a negative effect on South Africa's economy, resulting in a growing crisis. Finally, even the white minority that controlled the country realized the need to end apartheid. Between 1989 and 1994, President Frederik de Klerk, working with Nelson Mandela, took the necessary measures to bring to an end more than 50 years of segregation and injustices. In 1994, Nelson Mandela was elected as the first black president during the first free elections in the history of South Africa.

GLOSSARY

activist (AK-tiv-ist)—person who works for social or political change

apartheid (uh-PAR-tayt)—a former policy of racial segregation and discrimination in South Africa

BBC (BBC)—British Broadcasting Corporation; a British public service broadcaster that produces radio and TV shows

Boer (BORE)—a group of Dutch origin that settled in the territory of South Africa and Namibia in the 17th century. They were the dominant white minority in the territory until the end of apartheid in 1992.

boycott (BOY-kot)—to refuse to take part in something as a way of making a protest

charisma (kuh-RIZ-ma)—a special magnetic charm or appeal

colonialism (kuh-LOH-nee-uhl-iz-uhm)—the practice of gaining full or partial political control over another country and using it for economic gain

communist (KAHM-yuh-nist)—a person who believes in a system in which goods and property are owned by the government and shared in common

correspondence course (kor-uh-SPON-dunss KORSS)—a course of study in which students and teachers communicate by mail

demonstrate (DEM-uhn-strayt)—to join together with others to protest something

discrimination (dis-kri-muh-NAY-shuhn)—treating people unfairly because of their race, country of birth, or gender

domination (dom-uh-NAY-shuhn)—control over something through the use of strength and power

inferiority complex (in-FIHR-ee-or-i-tee KOM-pleks)—feeling like one has less value than someone else

inflation (in-FLAY-shuhn)—an increase in prices

negotiation (ni-GOH-shee-ay-shun)—talking to reach an agreement

occupation (awk-yuh-PAY-shuhn)—taking over and controlling another country with an army

oppress (oh-PRESS)—to treat someone in a cruel, unjust, and hard way

propaganda (prop-uh-GAN-duh)—information spread to try to influence the thinking of people; often not completely true or fair

radical (RAD-i-kuhl)—extreme compared to what most people think or do

reconciliation (REK-uhn-sil-ee-ay-shuhn)—restoring friendly relations between groups of people

regime (ri-ZHEEM)—the government in power

resignation (rez-ig-NAY-shuhn)—giving up a job, position, or office

revolutionary (rev-uh-LOO-shuhn-air-ee)—wanting to bring about major changes to the government of a country

segregation (seg-ruh-GAY-shuhn)—separating people because of their skin color

siege (SEEJ)—the surrounding of a city to cut off supplies and then wait for those inside to surrender

treason (TREE-zuhn)—the act of betraying one's country

underground (UHN-dur-grownd)—secret and done without government approval

DISCUSSION QUESTIONS

1.   Who do you think had the greatest influence on Nelson Mandela's political life? Explain your answer.

2.   Lazer Sidelsky, Mandela's first boss at the law firm, warns him that politics will only bring him problems. Do you agree with him? Do you think he was right? Discuss your thoughts with your classmates.

3.   What do think the differences are between passive resistance and active resistance? What do you think was the best way of opposing apartheid at that time? Illustrate your answer with an example from Mandela's life.

WRITING PROMPTS

1.   Imagine that you are a news reporter for your country in South Africa on the day of Mandela's freedom. Write an article about what happened from your country's perspective.

2.   Put yourself in the shoes of one of Robben Island's political prisoners. Write a brief message (that could fit inside a matchbox) to the common prisoners to organize a protest about one of your complaints.

3.   Imagine that, as an adult, Mandela writes a letter to himself as a child. What do you think he would say to himself?

ABOUT THE ILLUSTRATOR

Ignacio Segesso, from Buenos Aires, holds a degree in the visual arts. As an artist, he has held collective and individual exhibitions at comic conventions as well as in museums and galleries. He was selected in the Hall of Painting at the Quinquela Martin Museum and in the Contemporary Art Week (SAC) in Mar del Plata. He has worked as a colorist for *Patrulla 666*, which received an award at the 3rd Ibero-American Comics Fair. He won the first Proactiva award, which he received at the UNESCO headquarters in Paris. Currently he participates in the *Anthology of Argentine Heroes* and works on his project *Buenos Aires in Vignettes*, which was honored by the Buenos Aires City Government.

READ MORE

Capozzi, Suzy. *Nelson Mandela: From Prisoner to President.* Step into Reading. New York: Random House, 2016.

Kramer, Barbara. *Nelson Mandela.* National Geographic Kids. Washington, D.C.: National Geographic, 2014.

Malaspina, Ann. *Nelson Mandela: Fighting to Dismantle Apartheid.* Rebel with a Cause. New York: Enslow Publishing, 2017.

INTERNET SITES

Use Facthound to find Internet sites related to this book.

Visit *www.facthound.com*

Just type in 9781515791645 and go!

 Check out projects, games and lots more at
www.capstonekids.com

INDEX